KEYBOARD SIGHT READING

D1786249

Keyboard Sight Reading

Ellen Burmeister

University of Wisconsin—Madison

MAYFIELD PUBLISHING COMPANY

MOUNTAIN VIEW, CALIFORNIA

LONDON · TORONTO

To Ruth Clair,
whose artistry and intellectual openness
have been a lifelong influence.

Library of Congress Cataloging-in-Publication Data

Burmeister, Ellen.
  Keyboard sight reading / Ellen Burmeister.
    p. cm.
  Includes bibliographical references (p.   ) and index.
  ISBN 0–87484–981–0
  1. Sight reading (Music)   2. Piano—Instruction and study.
  I. Title.
MT236.B95   1991
786.2'1432—dc20   90–13440
                                                                CIP
                                                                MN

Manufactured in the United States of America
10 9 8 7 6 5 4 3 2 1

Mayfield Publishing Company
1240 Villa Street
Mountain View, California 94041

Sponsoring editor, Janet M. Beatty; managing editor, Linda Toy;
production editor, Sondra Glider; manuscript editor, Carole Crouse;
text and cover designer, Joan Greenfield;
music compositor, Ernie Mansfield, Music Graphics.

The text was set in 10/12 Aster by TypeLink, Inc., and printed
on 50# Finch Opaque by Bawden Printing.
Music on cover: Franz Schubert, Sonata in A major, Op. 120.

PREFACE

Anyone can become a competent sight reader within his or her acquired technical level, and basic techniques of reading *can* be learned. My goal in this book is to help players learn to become more flexible and to quickly assimilate what is on the page with rhythmic continuity.

The admonition "Work at it" seems to imply that keyboard players should simply do more reading; however, when practice reinforces what is already wrong, improvement is slow and laborious. In this text, I've identified many of the misunderstandings and errors that can contribute to weak reading, and I've offered solutions to help correct the problems.

Weak readers often avoid playing at sight simply because of their fear. Skill and courage are inseparable in sight reading. In addition to teaching the various skills involved in sight reading, this text helps students build the courage and self-reliance that are integral to successful reading.

Audience

The text is designed for any college-level keyboard player who has difficulty sight reading. Those who will benefit most are competent in some area of music, have fairly well-defined professional goals, and have some piano background. Although these students are a diverse group, common to all is a reading level not on a par with learned playing.

The concepts of the text will apply to any level of music, although few of the exercises use music at an elementary level. The text generally assumes a basic pianistic ability to play the easiest Kuhlau or Clementi sonatinas and Bach Little Preludes.

Although developed from a class designed specifically for reading, the text can handily supplement private or group piano study. It may be used from beginning to end, or certain portions may be extracted depending on the needs of the users. Each of the chapters moves progressively through introductory exercises to more difficult material.

Content

Weak reading inevitably includes one or more of the following deficiencies: lack of physical agility, inability to make instantaneous decisions, lack of flexibility, tense muscles, and lack of definite, continuous rhythm. I've organized the text around these specific weaknesses.

Chapter 1 begins with exercises designed to develop a reader's flexibility. Players who read with difficulty are often able to execute learned pieces or exercises quite skillfully. Often they have learned to rely on the reassurance that comes with many repetitions. Chapter 1 helps students instead to rely on instincts, go with impressions, and take chances.

Fearful pianists almost always play with held breath, worried expressions, and intense, fixed eyes. Chapter 2 calls attention to these tendencies and suggests ways to overcome them.

Inert, inactive eyes that remain locked on one detail indicate a passive player who is afraid to continue until every note is perfect. Chapter 3 encourages players to look ahead.

Weak readers seldom relate the upcoming notes to those they have just played. Contact is the basis for dexterity, balance, efficiency, and voice-leading. Chapter 4 surveys fingering practices upon which contact depends. It is the basis for breaking the habit of looking down.

Reading note by note clearly inhibits continuous reading. Chapter 5 weans the reader from reading individual notes by stressing the intervals between notes rather than the notes' names. Transposition by clefs and figured bass is used to hone these ideas. Also stressed is perceiving note groups and directions of musical fragments impressionistically rather than identifying all the individual components.

Harmonic reading is possibly the single most important key to reading. In Chapter 6, readers practice replacing reading the individual tones that make up the chord with seeing a harmony as a single entity.

Based on principles introduced in preceding chapters, Chapter 7 gives additional hints to help with score reading. These include handling doublings, omissions, redistributions, and other procedural instructions. Examples progress from piano pieces expanded into score form to a Haydn symphony.

Rather than devoting a separate chapter to the very important concept of rhythm, I've stressed rhythm throughout the text. Using a metronome, playing on principal beats, counting aloud, and playing for a conductor compel a continuous beat, and exercises throughout provide practice in each of these areas.

Using This Text

The exercises are presented in an order that seemed sensible to me, but it may not suit everyone. Some instructors may prefer to skip around in the book, isolating those exercises that apply directly to their students. Others may progress from beginning to end. Although this text represents my convictions about basic reading techniques, any methodology must be balanced with spontaneity and individuality.

The class level for which the exercises were designed was a group of four students, each at a keyboard. Fewer than four students is seldom satisfactory, and it is *very* important that students have their own keyboards. Once an exercise has been introduced and practiced, students should apply the principle to sight reading of additional practice music. Improvement depends on understanding the purpose behind the exercises and applying that understanding to practice.

Acknowledgments

I wish to thank the reviewers of this text, whose suggestions, reactions, and honesty were of great help: Martha Baker, California State University, Fullerton; Thomas Fritz, University of Nebraska, Lincoln; Joyce Grill, University of Wisconsin, Lacrosse; Christopher Hepp, University of Kansas; Janet Mann, University of Utah; and E. Gregory Nagode, Southern Methodist University. Special thanks are due Eva Wright, Madison, Wisconsin, and Marcia Roberts, DePauw University, who are always an inspiration.

I'd also like to thank Katherine Younger, who not only ably and patiently typed the manuscript but also kept me organized, and the people at Mayfield Publishing Company who worked on this project: Jan Beatty, sponsoring editor; Debby Horowitz, product manager; Sondra Glider, production editor; Pamela Trainer, permissions editor; and Carole Crouse, copyeditor. I would also like to recognize the piano students with whom this material has been used, and whose progress confirmed that we were on the right track.

CONTENTS

CHAPTER ONE

Flexibility 1

Concentration   2
Improvisation   9
Bass Lines   11
Free Transpositions   13
Score   17
Keyboard Feel   19

CHAPTER TWO

Eyes and Breathing 20

Soft Eyes   20
Breathing   21

CHAPTER THREE

Eyes in Motion 24

Playing from Recall   24
Scanning   28
Not Looking Down   31
Peripheral and Agile Vision   35
Vocal Literature   35
Piano, Four Hands   40
Scores   44

CHAPTER FOUR

Contact 51

Substitution   52
Slides   54
Unorthodox Crossings   56
Balanced Independence   58
Systematic Releases   64
Hidden Repeated Notes   64

Leaps   78
Play-Move-Place   78
Play-Move-Place Legato   84

CHAPTER FIVE

Horizontal Intervals 86

Horizontal Reading   86
Exercises in Horizontal Interval Reading   87
Examples for Horizontal Reading   88
Transposition of the Tenor Line   90
Transposition by Clefs   95
Clef Substitution   96
C Clefs   100
Figured Bass   107
Keyboard Feel   110

CHAPTER SIX

Vertical Reading 111

Harmonic Reading   111
Composite of Skills   133
Different Perceptions of One Piece   133

CHAPTER SEVEN

Score Reading 138

Reduction of Clutter   138
Redistribution of Parts   144
Omissions   147
Expansion-Contraction   151
Score   160

ANNOTATED BIBLIOGRAPHY   165

CHAPTER ONE

Flexibility

Skillful and effective piano reading requires independence, self-reliance, suppleness of spirit, elasticity of technique, and adaptability. The goal is to go forward accurately with continuous rhythm.

Fluent sight readers are flexible. They are aptly described by the definitions of *flexible* given in the *Oxford English Dictionary:*

1. Capable of being bent; pliant

2. Willing to yield to pressure

3. Susceptible to modification or adaptation to various purposes or conditions

4. Not rigid.

Weak readers nearly always display the opposite characteristics: stiffness, rigidity, lack of pliancy, inadaptability, inability to modify as needed.

This text in its entirety treats inflexibility by exploring very specific barriers to fluent sight reading. Figured bass and C clefs will encourage intervallic reading. Insistence on continuous rhythm will help the reader to overcome fear. Reading by large harmonic design will remove the habit of reading individual notes. Not looking down will encourage self-reliance. Throughout the book, the player will be asked to see the music, feel the keyboard, and sense the body in new ways. All are part of the treatment for inflexibility.

The exercises in Chapter 1, however, are much more general than the exercises in succeeding chapters. They require the reader to play simultaneously with various distractions, such as conversing while playing, intermingling reading and improvising, emulating a given style, reading music in an innovative notation, and scanning a score while part of an ensemble. The aim of the activities, besides developing the flexibility necessary for competent reading, is to heighten concentration.

CONCENTRATION

Play Figures 1.1 and 1.2 while engaging in one of the following activities:

1. Describe the attire of various people in the room.

2. Converse with another person. The conversation must be active.

3. If there is a large clock in the room, tell the time to the exact minute or second. Otherwise, look at your watch.

4. Stand in front of the piano with the music on top and play.

5. Repeat item 4, but now occasionally look across the piano as if at a class of children.

6. Have someone hold a large still-life poster (one you have not previously seen) to the side. Describe the picture in detail.

Suggested metronome markings are not given. Each student should find the tempo that best suits his or her level. The important point is continuity.

These exercises can also be applied to music already learned, such as scales, arpeggios, exercises, improvisation, or memorized music. As an additional exercise, play with eyes closed.

FIGURE 1.1 Johann Hässler, from *Der Tonkreis*

FIGURE 1.1, continued

FIGURE 1.1, continued

FIGURE 1.1, continued

FIGURE 1.1, continued

FIGURE 1.1, continued

FIGURE 1.2 Alberto Ginastera, *Sadness (Triste)*
Reprinted from *Twelve American Preludes*, vol. I, no. 2.
Copyright © by Carl Fischer, Inc., New York.
Copyright renewed. International copyright
secured. Reprint by permission.
All rights reserved.

IMPROVISATION

Since sight reading deals with a printed page and improvising deals with aural perceptions, the two skills may seem to be unrelated to each other. In fact, however, they make a number of the same demands on the pianist. Those demands may seem more obvious in the skill of improvisation. Reading, because of its attention to the printed page, often tends to block some of them out. The demands include, but are not limited to, the following:

1. Have courage.
2. Have conviction.
3. Trust your musical instincts.
4. Insist on rhythmic continuity.
5. Understand the harmonic foundation.
6. Perceive the music's direction.
7. Go with musical impressions.
8. Perceive the style.
9. Rely on your tactile sense.
10. Be inventive.

The great bassist Richard Davis, who is equally at home in jazz improvisation and classical music, said to a piano major in his Black Music Ensemble class, "Don't be afraid of mistakes. Classical musicians are always afraid of mistakes." On the one hand, reading competence requires accuracy. On the other hand, even the best readers make mistakes. The goal is to learn to play past mistakes without interrupting the flow of the music. When mistakes occur, make the most of them.

For the incomplete fragments in Figure 1.3, improvise suitable extensions and conclusions, using your imagination within the musical guidelines established by the fragment. The only error is doing nothing. Imagine that you are accompanying a soloist and the page-turner fails to turn the page—what do you do? Stop? Only on pain of death. Stopping is never allowed, so you must fake, vamp, and improvise as best you can, still listening to the soloist. The examples given here do not include accompaniments with a solo part, but a bad page-turn can be created and practiced with a fellow student.

FIGURE 1.3

(continued)

FIGURE 1.3, continued

FIGURE 1.3, continued

BASS LINES

Improvise a melody, a descant, or a harmony, deriving a right-hand style from the bass and left-hand lines in Figure 1.4.

FIGURE 1.4

(continued)

FIGURE 1.4, continued

FREE TRANSPOSITIONS

Figures 1.5, 1.6, and 1.7 were designed by an experienced classroom teacher who was experimenting with ways to make transposition as easy and accessible as possible. Since no pitches are specified, the player is completely freed of note transposition. Everything else—rhythm, scale degree, and chords—is specified without relation to pitch names. The transpositions feel natural and easy without clefs or transposition intervals to think about. Play the songs in as many different keys as possible.

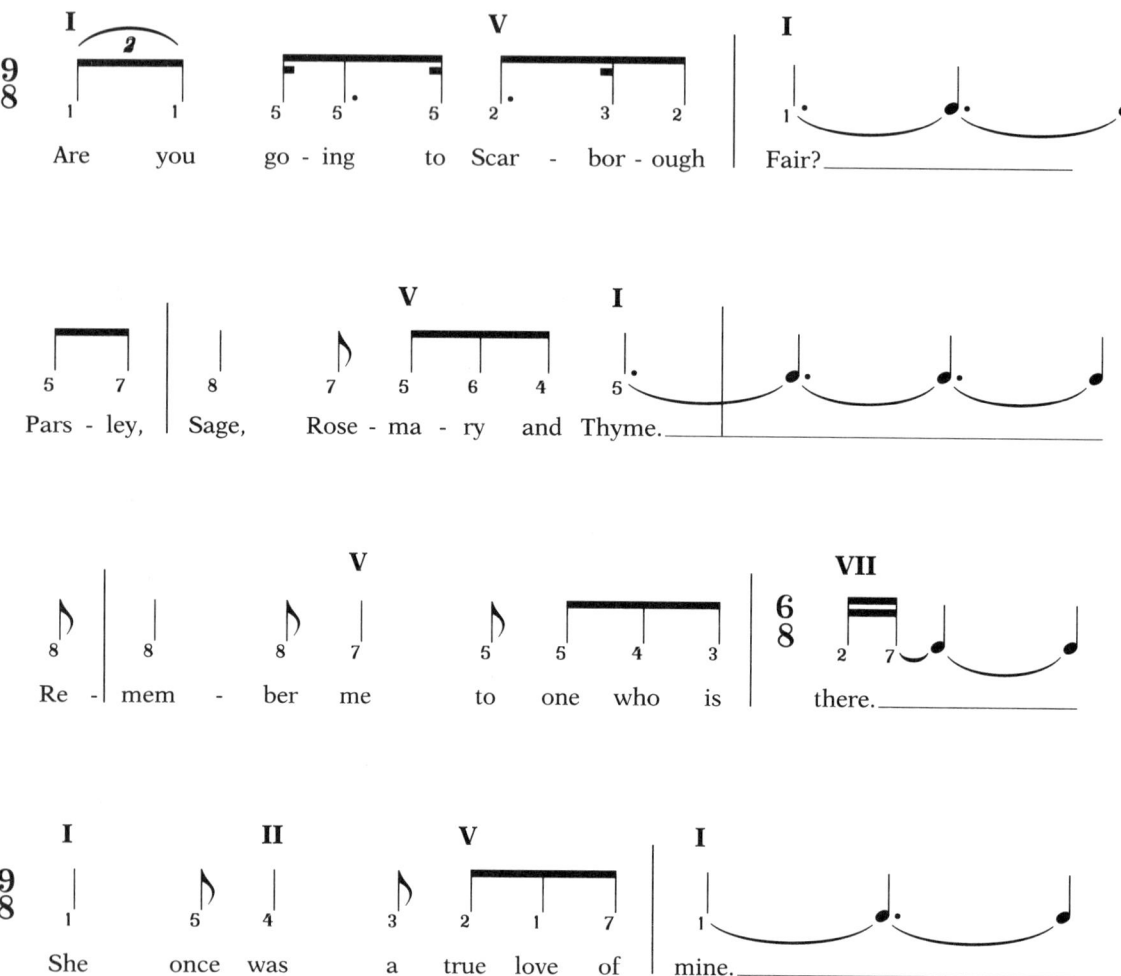

Tell her to find me an acre of land.
Parsley, Sage, Rosemary and Thyme.
Between the salt water and the sea strand.
Then she'll be a true love of mine.

FIGURE 1.5 *Scarborough Fair*, arr. Carolyn Udell

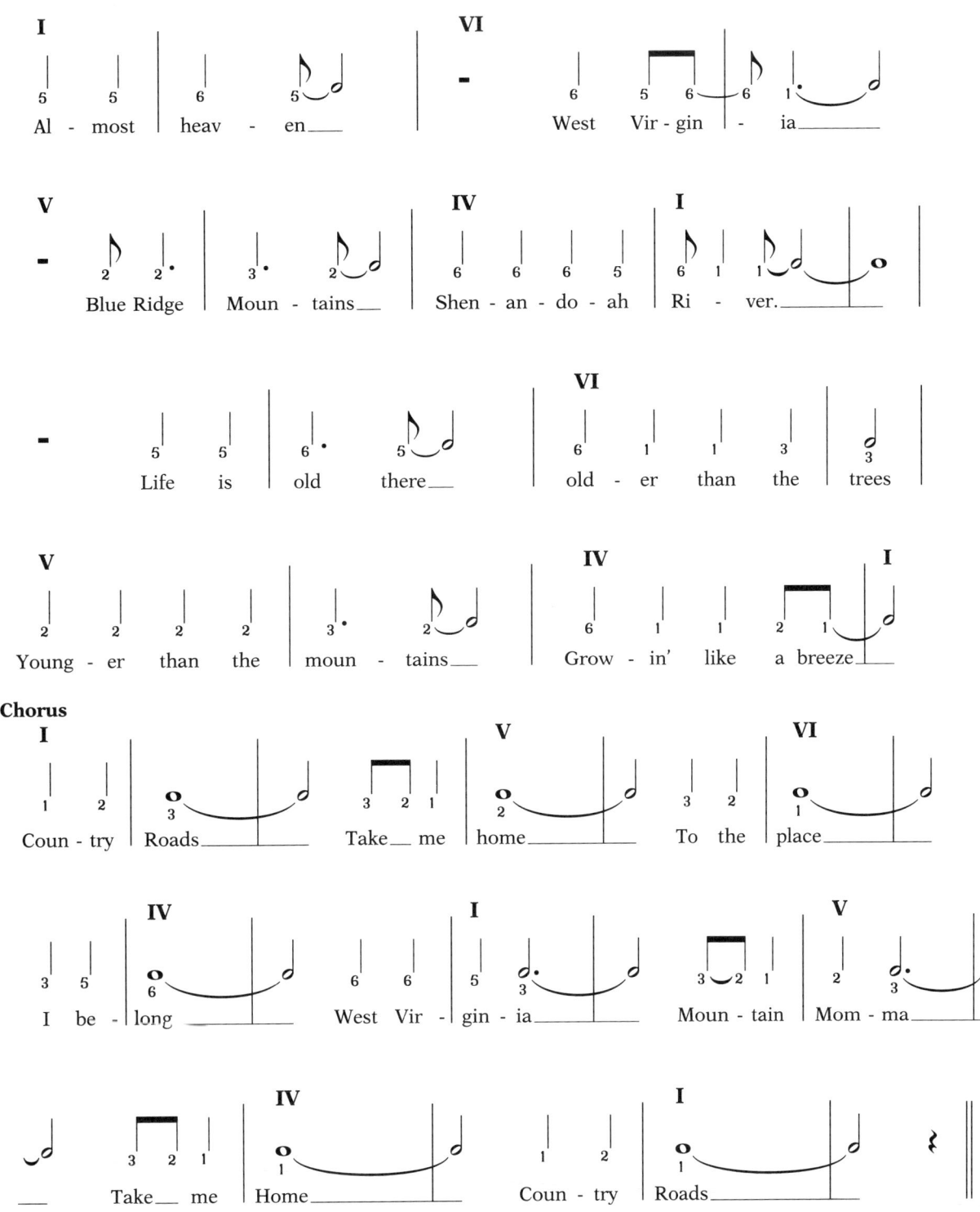

FIGURE 1.6 *Country Roads*, arr. Carolyn Udell

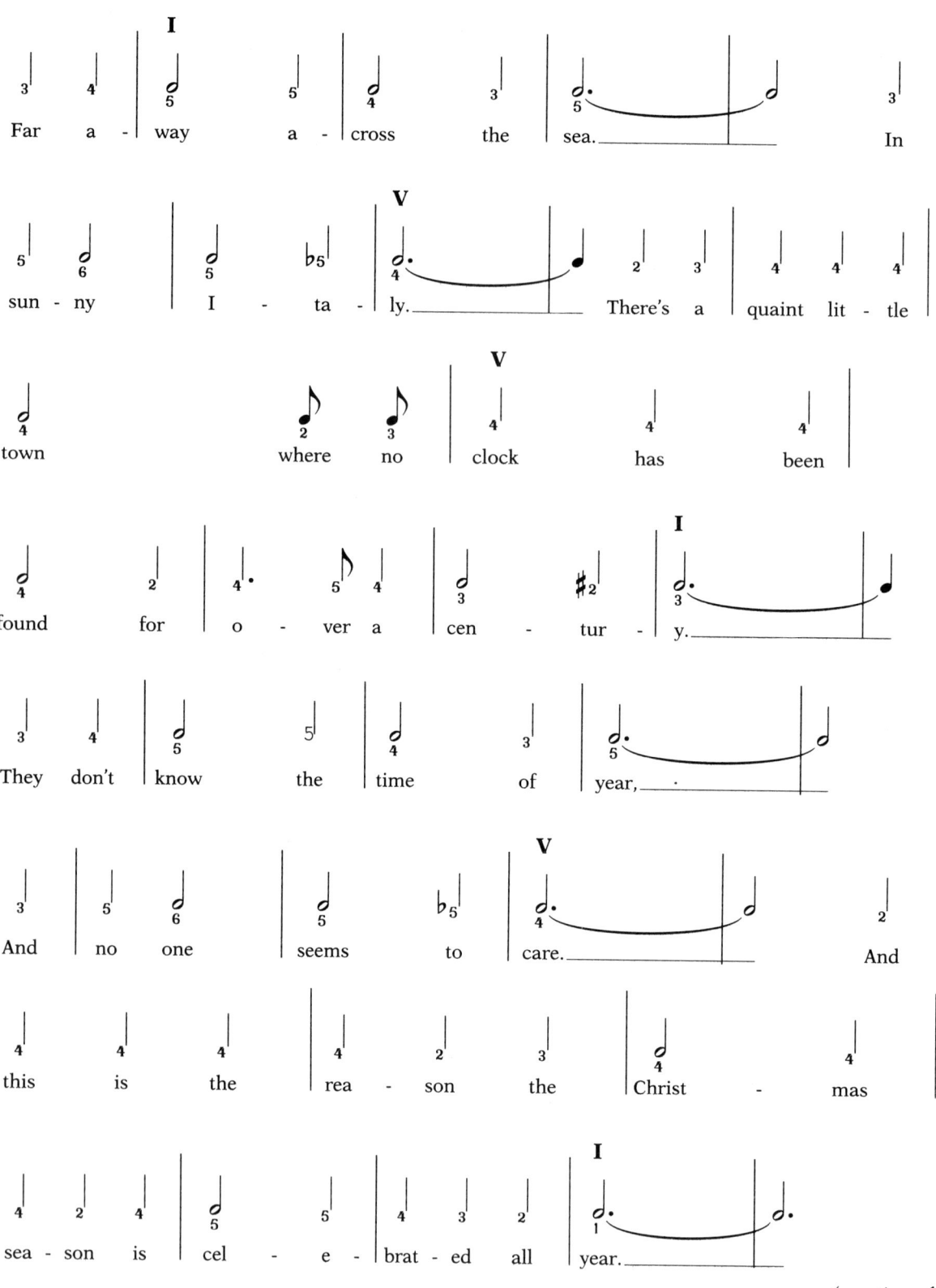

FIGURE 1.7   *Buon Natale,* arr. Carolyn Udell

(continued)

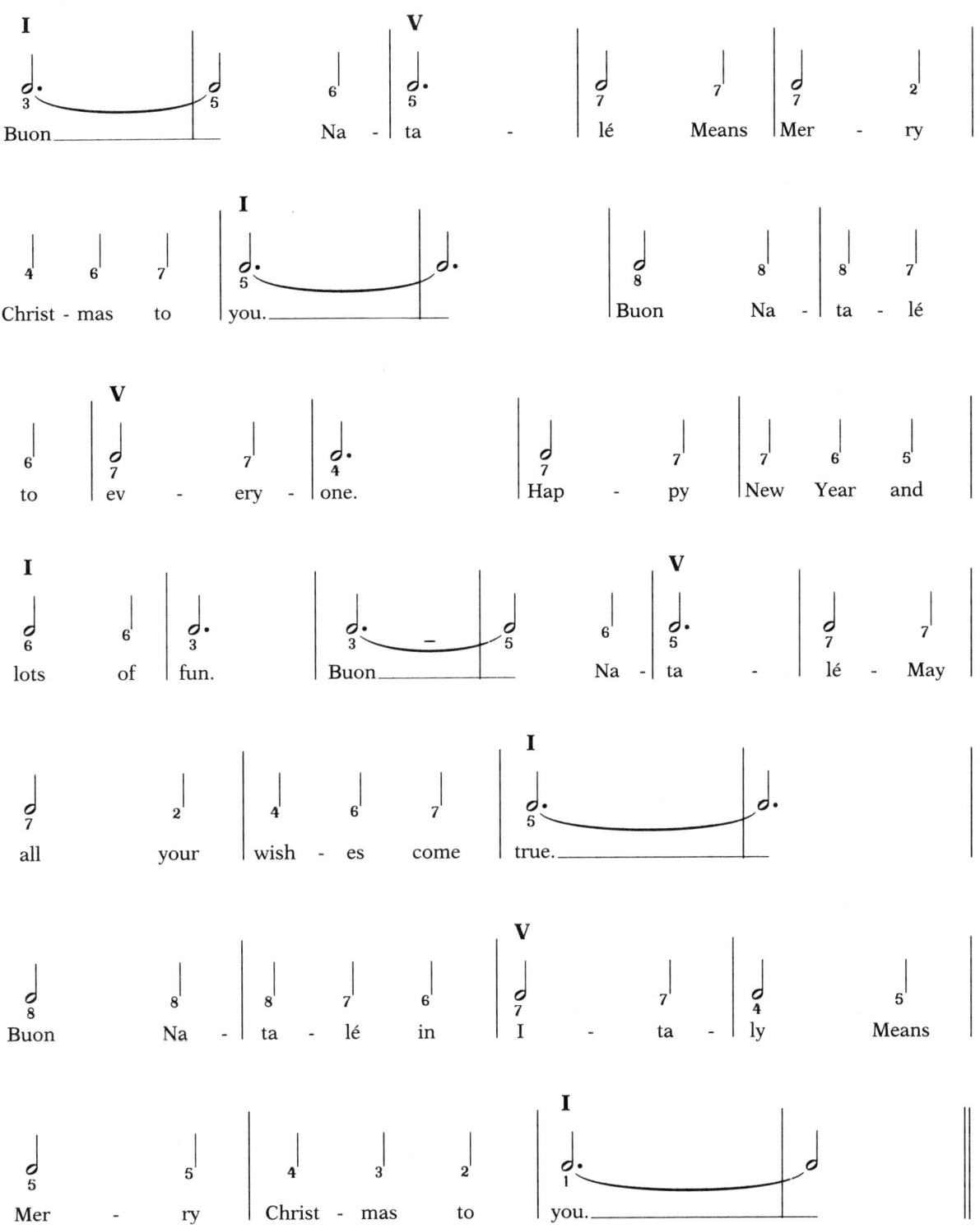

FIGURE 1.7, continued

SCORE

Do as many different things as possible with the scored version of the fugue in Figure 1.8. For example, (1) play as a trio, one player to a part; (2) scan the other two parts while playing one; (3) recite downbeat harmonies, first without playing, then while playing; (4) play one line in the right hand while chording downbeat harmonies in the left hand, then reverse; (5) play one part in each hand; (6) look up the original and work with the keyboard version and this scored expansion side by side; (7) play the entire score after first determining distribution of the middle line between the hands. Other ideas?

(continued)

FIGURE 1.8   J. S. Bach, *The Well-Tempered Clavier*, Fuga II
Reprinted by permission of Belwin-Mills Publishing
Company c/o CPP/Belwin, Inc., Miami, FL 33014.

FIGURE 1.8, continued

KEYBOARD FEEL

The mysterious faculty called "keyboard feel" can be acquired and improved at any level of playing. Some people, especially particularly talented keyboard players, exhibit an uncanny knack for "knowing the keyboard." Their hands seem to effortlessly find their own way around the keys. It is not, however, a skill reserved for the gifted few. Although keyboard feel is not easily taught, there are paths that will lead to an awareness of the sensation. Later, the text deals with some of these approaches in detail, particularly in Chapter 4, "Contact."

This is a quick introduction to gaining a sense of "keyboard feel." Choose music you have already learned by heart, and play it with eyes closed or looking well above the keyboard. The music you choose may be very simple, such as five-finger patterns in various keys; slightly more difficult, such as Hanon exercises in different keys; or much more difficult, such as scales and arpeggios or even a memorized piece. In each case, the tempo may need to be slower than usual. If, at first, you tend to take occasional peeks at the keyboard, play even slower, hesitating, if necessary, to find the next note. Gradually increase the tempo.

By practicing different passages repeatedly in this way, the fingers, hand, and arm will begin to feel the music as soon as you think it or, in the case of sight reading, see it.

CHAPTER TWO

Eyes and Breathing

SOFT EYES

When reading, the eyes are the body's initial contact with the music. It is important, therefore, to be aware of their movement so that you can use your eyes to their fullest advantage. To do so, it is fundamental to explore the concept of "soft eyes."[1]

When reading music, the eyes should rest only fleetingly on any one thing, floating lightly from harmony to harmony or from pattern to pattern. At the same time, your gaze must have an invisible but elastic tether to the point on the page at which you are playing. Various musical exercises are included later in the text to guide you in grasping this idea, but the following exercise helps describe the process without the responsibility of playing music.

1. Read aloud a paragraph or a poem with a helper standing directly behind you. As you read, the helper will advance an object, such as a pencil, at eye level. The instant you can perceive the object, stop reading, even if you are in mid-syllable.

2. Measure exactly where the object was located in relation to your head when you stopped reading. Still facing forward, gradually move your gaze as far toward the object as possible. Softly hold your gaze there for two or three seconds, and then return it to the page in front of you.

3. Now repeat steps 1 and 2 from the opposite side.

4. Return to step 1 again but from the original side. Most people perceive the advancing object earlier than they did the first time.

5. Experiment with objects of different colors to explore how early each new color can be identified.

Before reading the next page, focus intently for a few seconds on the X in the middle of the page. Concentrate on the diagonals and the four V's at each end of the diagonals.

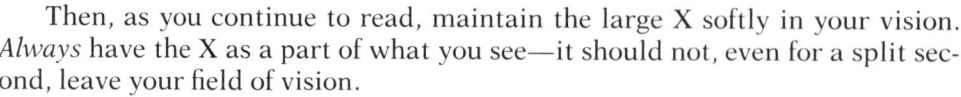

Then, as you continue to read, maintain the large X softly in your vision. *Always* have the X as a part of what you see—it should not, even for a split second, leave your field of vision.

Notice that while you focused intently on the center of the X, the surrounding words were blocked from your vision. This is called "hard eyes" and frequently happens when you stare at a chord in a desperate attempt to get the notes right. Several beats of time are lost, destroying rhythm and continuity.

While proceeding to read with the X in your vision, you should have no difficulty reading the entire page; peripheral vision works well. Notice also that you read with a slow but constant sweeping motion of the eyes. This is called "soft eyes" and must be in effect at all times while reading.

Now read the page four more times:

1. Maintain the square–X–circle diagonal in your vision.

2. Maintain the asterisk–X–triangle diagonal in your vision.

3. Move the eyes softly from one symbol to another while reading.

4. Maintain all five symbols in your vision as you read.

Read Figure 2.1 on p. 22, following the same exercises.

Variation: While playing, glance quickly at one of the symbols and back to the point you are reading. Do this several times throughout the piece.

BREATHING

Take notice also of breathing activity. Most inefficient readers hold their breath, particularly when in difficulty, and many hold their breath even as they approach the piano. Even a fluent reader will feel the effects of held breath. Eva Wright, a colleague of the author's who is an outstanding reader, recently stated, "When I'm blocked, it's inevitably because my breathing has stopped or because my abdominal muscles are tight." Held breath has many deleterious effects on the body, such as increased heart rate, elevated blood pressure, and reduced supply of oxygen to the brain. "Of all the things you can do to enhance your [playing], attending to your breathing may well be the most effective."[2]

A student, asked to write down body response to held breath while reading, offered the cluster arrangement shown in Figure 2.2 on p. 23.[3]

While working through the text, give yourself constant reminders to breathe regularly and to relax the abdominal muscles until your body is in the habit of doing so. Include breathing in the day's piano warm-ups. Practice five-finger exercises, such as Hanon's, with alternating inhalation-exhalation patterns.

Practice scales and arpeggios, inhaling on the ascent and exhaling on the descent, and then repeat the scales and arpeggios, reversing the breathing pattern.

Practice some of the text's examples with purposely held breath and tight abdominal muscles. Then play with soft eyes, regular breathing, and released abdominal muscles, and describe the difference in sound. Play both ways for a musical friend without first explaining the exercise. Ask your friend to describe the difference in sound.

FIGURE 2.1 John La Montaine, *Copycats*, "Winter Winds"
Copyright © 1957 by Summy-Birchard.

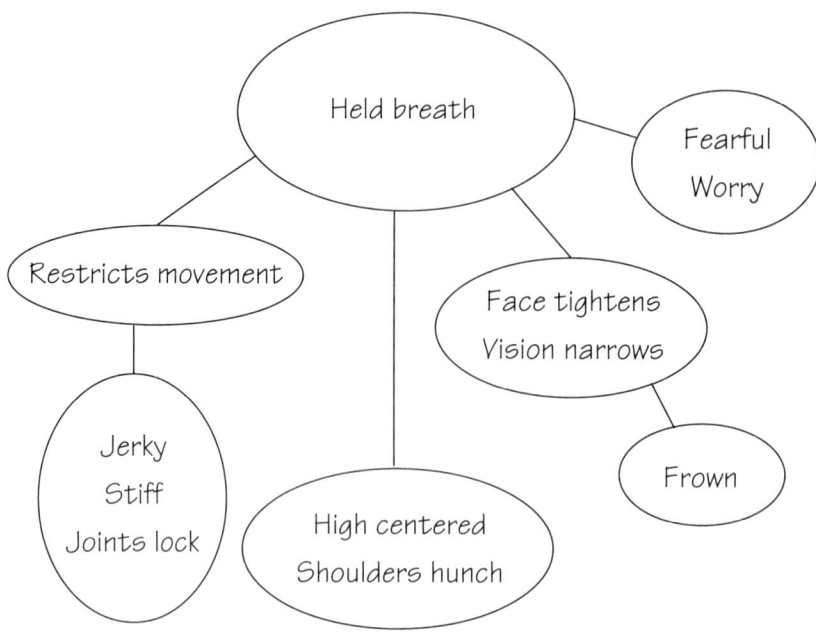

FIGURE 2.2

NOTES

1. Sally Swift, *Centered Riding* (New York: St. Martin's Press, 1985), pp. 10–11.
2. Denise McCluggage, *The Centered Skier* (New York: Bantam Books, 1983), p. 136.
3. Gabriele Lusser Rico, *Writing the Natural Way: Using Right-Brain Techniques to Release Your Expressive Powers* (Los Angeles: J. P. Tarcher, 1983).

CHAPTER THREE

Eyes in Motion

PLAYING FROM RECALL

Critical to successful reading is the ability to look ahead. What one has just read is to be performed from recall as the eyes perceive the next pattern or chord. Most players who have difficulty reading at sight have developed the habit of visually locking onto the chord or pattern they are waiting to play. Their eyes do not move forward until those notes have been executed. Old habits die hard and occasionally recur. To change them requires patient and assiduous attention.

The leapfrog process of playing one thing while seeing another requires both skill and courage. While lack of technique is a handicap, by far the bigger handicap is lack of courage, confidence, and conviction. Leapfrogging can be the introduction to *allowing* oneself to play at sight as opposed to *forcing* oneself to play at sight. The player is being asked to greet the unknown, and many do not feel secure enough to take such a chance, blaming instead their supposed lack of technique for their inadequacy in reading ahead.

In actual reading, this leapfrog process occurs very quickly. The exercises for Figures 3.1, 3.2, and 3.3 map out in slow motion how it occurs. To help you in reading ahead, a second person might cover the pattern being played, forcing your gaze ahead of your fingers.

In the various stages of the exercises, only a few things should be of concern:

1. Your eyes must move rhythmically from group to group.

2. Continuity is essential.

3. Note the direction of line (up, down, and so on).

4. Observe the large rhythm of each measure (in this piece every half-measure).

5. When in doubt, do something.

6. Do not look down at your hands under any circumstances!

You need not worry about

1. Fingerings
2. Note accuracy
3. Small rhythms (for example, discriminating between dotted eighths and double-dotted eighths)
4. Mistakes

Even such musical refinements as legato, phrasing, and dynamics are secondary in importance at this stage. They grow in importance as the level of reading improves.

While practicing exercises A, B, and C, let your eyes move evenly and rhythmically from group to group, staying always on the music.

A. *Right Hand Alone* (Figure 3.1): By the second eighth of each measure, your eyes should be on the next measure while playing the group just read. If your eyes are reluctant to move ahead that quickly, have someone cover the measure on the second eighth.

Right hand

FIGURE 3.1

B. *Left Hand Alone* (Figure 3.2): The same process applies, with the eyes moving to the following measure by the fifth eighth of each measure.

Left hand

FIGURE 3.2

C. *Hands Together* (Figure 3.3): Now the eyes will move vertically every half-measure as well as horizontally. Remember to move your eyes rhythmically. They will be in almost constant motion. If it is difficult to establish rhythmic eye movement, have someone cover every half-measure on the second and fourth beats.

The music of Figure 3.4 is naturally segmented by the rests. This gives the reader more time to organize, but the time must be used wisely; that is, the eyes must have moved *before* the rest, as the arrows indicate. The silence can then be used to confirm accuracy before playing.

FIGURE 3.3   John La Montaine, *Plaintive*
Reprinted from *Twelve Relationships, Opus 10*.
Copyright © 1965 by Carl Fischer Publishing.

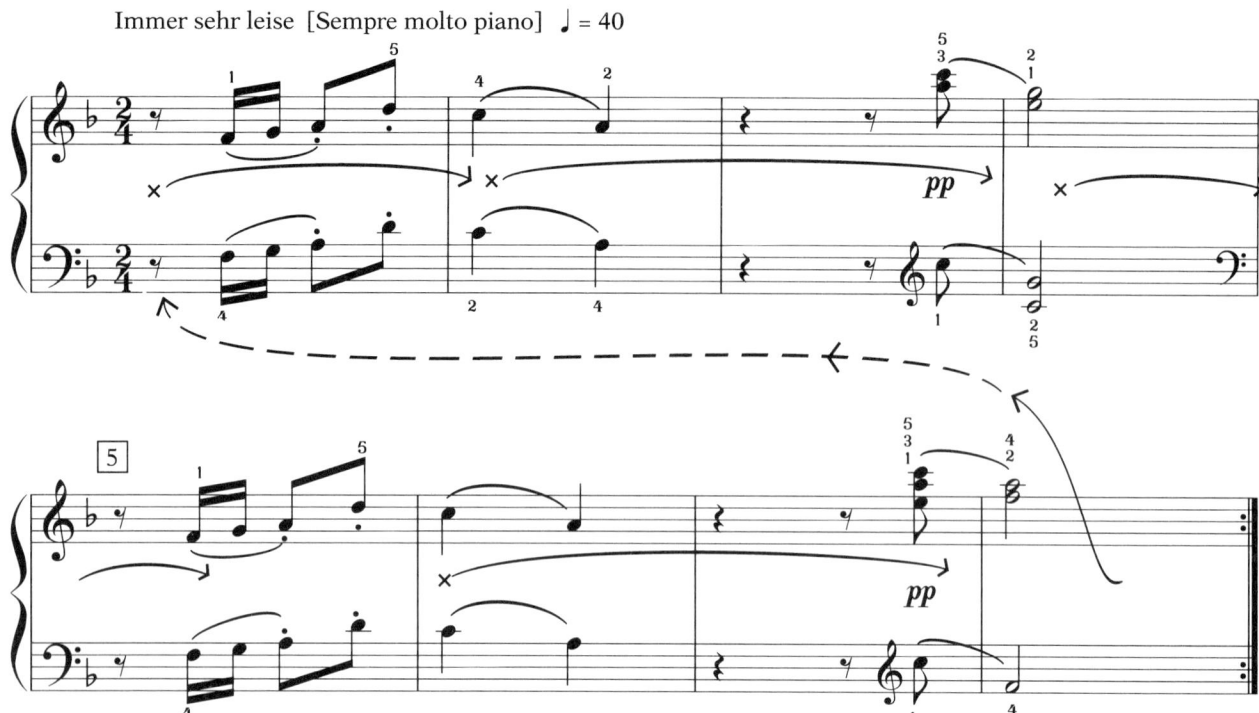

Immer sehr leise [Sempre molto piano] ♩ = 40

FIGURE 3.4   Robert Schumann, *Cuckoo in Hiding*

SCANNING

When playing a piece at sight, it is important to conduct a quick scan of the music to notice its various landmarks. We will use Figure 3.7 as an example. Going through the following exercise will take several minutes, but keep in mind that in actual performance, scanning occurs in a matter of seconds.

1. First, chord or cluster; that is, play all notes in a measure at once, including nonharmonic tones. Take time to practice this on the keyboard (see Figure 3.5). Chording-clustering on the keyboard is a valuable learning tool; it may also be effective when rehearsed silently.

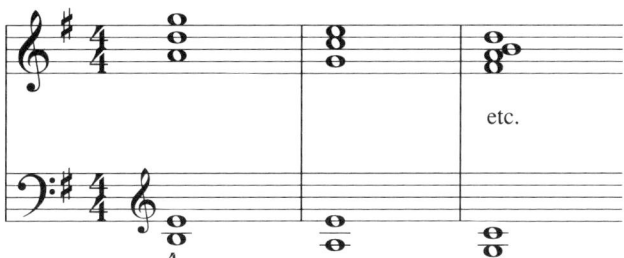

FIGURE 3.5

2. Scan for bass-line movement (see Figure 3.6). Note the following:
   a. Whether the bass line skips or moves diatonically
   b. The direction of skip
   c. The precise interval of skip
   d. The color of keys outlining the skip
   e. Clef changes—that is, during measures 3, 4, 6

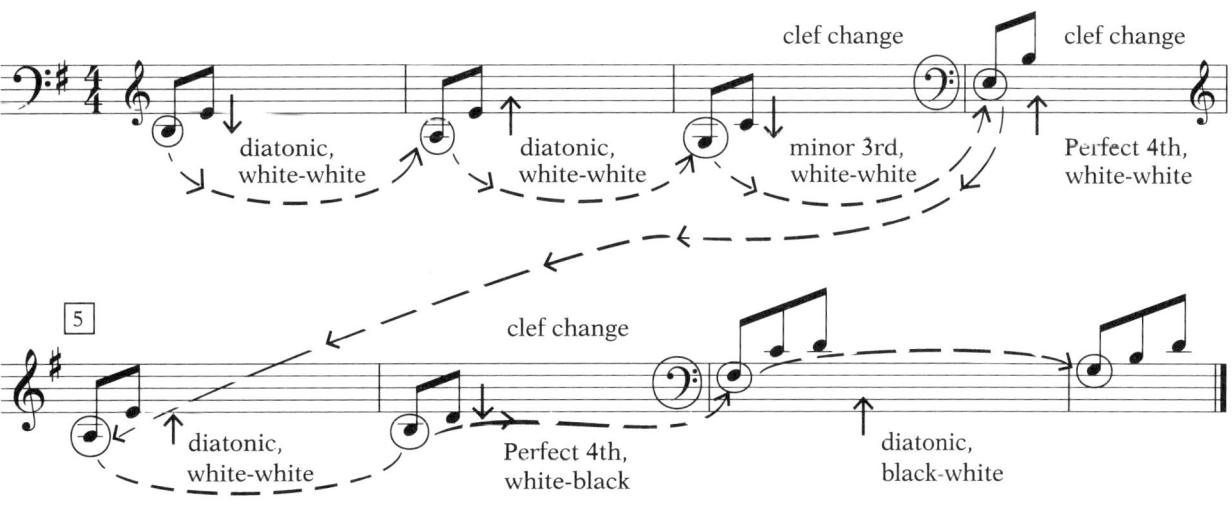

FIGURE 3.6

3. After reading Figure 3.7 once or twice (do not wait for perfection), read while simultaneously doing one of the following:
   a. Follow a conductor.
   b. Establish eye contact with others in the room.
   c. Have someone hold a large object at an 80-degree angle to the side; describe the object as you play.
   d. Have someone hold up several objects; as you play, identify how many objects there are.

   By the half note of each measure, your eyes should have moved to the next measure.

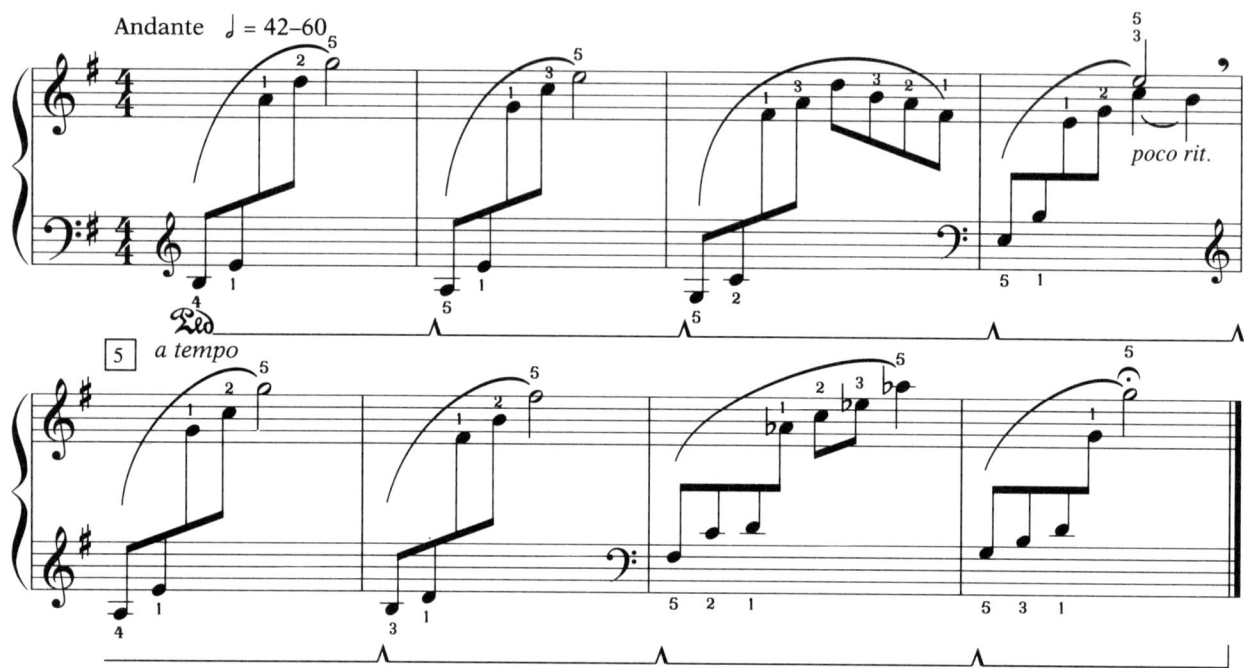

FIGURE 3.7   Walter Finlayson, *Sketches for Piano,* "Stars"
Copyright © MCMLX by Edward B. Marks Music Corporation.

As a second exercise, a quick, sixty-second scan of Figure 3.8 reveals these landmarks:

1. The piece is chordal.

2. The harmonic movement is mostly diatonic.

3. There is a change of meters.

4. In the last line, the left hand moves.

5. The pedal is important.

When playing the piece the first time, remind your eyes to scan ahead to identify new patterns before it is time to play them.

FIGURE 3.8   Walter Finlayson, *Sketches for Piano*, "The Peacock"
Copyright © MCMLX by Edward B. Marks Music Corporation.

NOT LOOKING DOWN

To read successfully, it is crucial to avoid looking down at the keyboard. Competent readers rarely look down while playing. Weak readers look down frequently, often twice or more for the same harmony. That habit must be changed. It occurs because the player is insecure about finding the next notes to be played and because he or she needs to confirm the notes just read by making sure the hands are in the correct place.

Some solutions to the problem have already been suggested. Soft eyes, peripheral vision, scanning, and recall all contribute to the player's security.

Figures 3.9, 3.10, and 3.11 (on pp. 32–35) appear in ascending order of difficulty. When reading them, apply the preceding techniques. In addition, maintain an even chin level. Rigorously follow the direction "Do not, under any circumstances, look at the keyboard." As with any rule, there are exceptions; in the first two pieces, possible exceptions are marked by asterisks, large ones for "probably necessary to look down" and small ones for "possibly necessary to look down." Have someone count the number of times you look down as you are reading the pieces (force of habit will usually prevail at first). Then count for yourself the number of times you look down.

The immediate goal is to maintain an even chin level. This practice allows the eyes to move freely from measure to measure and around the page, making full use of peripheral vision. Notice that the directions in the preceding paragraph suggest an "even" chin level. That does not mean that the chin must be parallel to the floor. Try slanting your chin toward the black notes. Notice that your eyes can then glance at the keys without up-and-down head movement, and they also have free range over the music.

There is an apparent contradiction between not looking down under any circumstances and maintaining an even chin level so that you can just glance at the keyboard. This can be resolved by pointing out that the worst, unforgivable, and most amateurish sin is repeatedly moving the head up and down. If it becomes necessary to check the keyboard, a mere glance of the eyes is permissible. It gradually becomes less and less necessary to glance down at all.

Remember, too, that there is a considerable difference between reading at uprights and reading at grand pianos. The distance from music to keyboard is much greater at the latter; the chin level should be lowered so that, when necessary, the eyes can move easily from music to keyboard. Inexperienced players will be particularly affected by this and should be cautioned to make adjustments in chin level.

Other aids in resolving this problem will be directly addressed in the chapter on contact and fingerings as well as throughout the book.

As preparation for the three following pieces, read the preceding pieces once more without looking down. Then proceed to Figures 3.9, 3.10, and 3.11.

Before reading Figure 3.10 without looking down, scan to do the following:

1. Notice key—think of white notes used instead of flatted notes.

2. Check for accidentals (measures 10–14 and 19–20).

3. Observe that the piece is a canon.

FIGURE 3.9   Darius Milhaud, *A Child Loves*, "Flowers"
Copyright © MCMXLIV by Hal Leonard Publishing.

FIGURE 3.9, continued

FIGURE 3.10   César Franck, *Kanon*
© 1942 by C. F. Peters. Used by permission.

FIGURE 3.11   Friedrich Burgmuller, *The Gypsies*

PERIPHERAL AND AGILE VISION

Vocal Literature

Soft eyes and peripheral vision are called into use when accompanying soloists, since it is necessary to be visually aware of more than the accompaniment. The eyes must move with agility, scanning the soloist's part in addition to the piano score and even at times seeing the soloist. The need to play from recall becomes more obvious and prevalent than in piano score.

Vocal music is a good introduction to accompanying and score reading for two reasons: It has only one additional layer (the vocal line and lyrics) to read, and it lies very near to the piano accompaniment; and one can practice even without a soloist by singing or speaking the lyrics while playing the accompaniment, thus ensuring that the vocal line is also being read. The rest of the pieces in this chapter progress through easy recitatives to somewhat more difficult songs, to a Haydn symphony in open score, and finally to a Bach fugue in open score.

In the five recitatives and songs that follow:

1. Play the accompaniment and sing or speak the lyrics (it may be necessary to practice the accompaniment first).

2. Accompany a soloist. Keep the soloist in your peripheral vision.

FIGURE 3.12   G. F. Handel, *Messiah*, "Unto which of the angels said He"

FIGURE 3.13   G. F. Handel, *Messiah*, "Then shall the eyes
of the blind be opened"

FIGURE 3.14   G. F. Handel, *Messiah*, "Thy rebuke hath broken His heart"

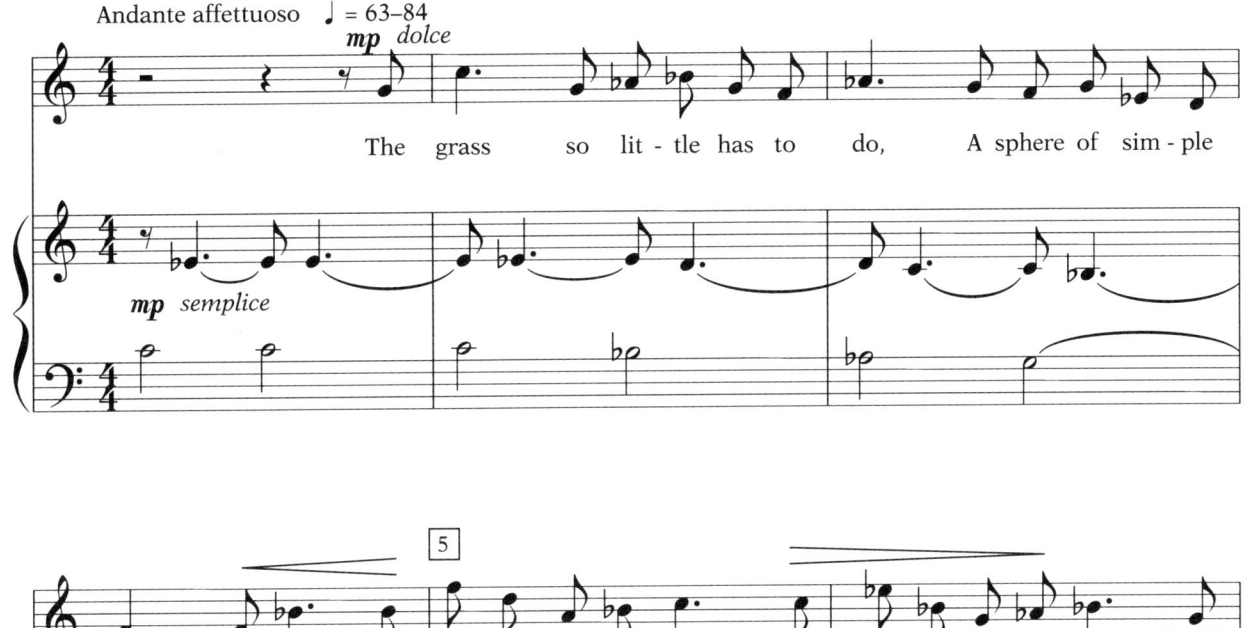

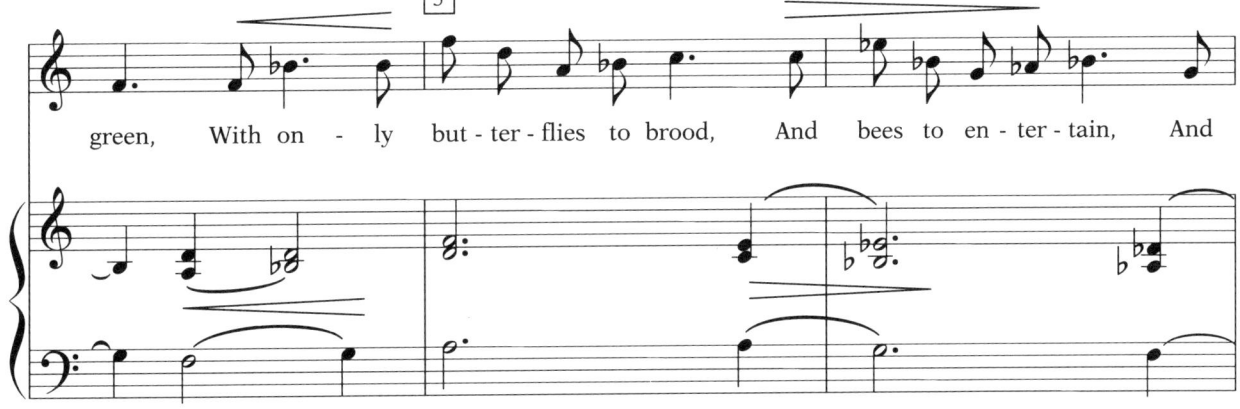

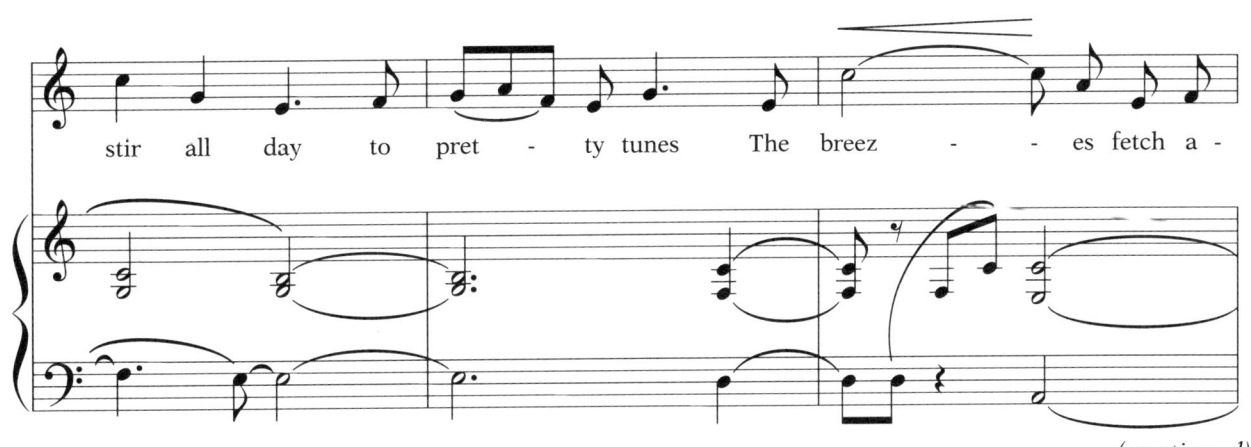

(continued)

FIGURE 3.15 Vincent Persichetti, *Emily Dickinson Songs*,
"The Grass," Op. 77, No. 4
© 1958 Elkan-Vogel, Inc. Used by permission of the publisher.
Sole representative—Theodore Presser Company.

FIGURE 3.15, continued

Poco agitato ♩ = 50–60

Now wild geese re - turn...

What draws them cry - ing,

FIGURE 3.16 Robert Birch, *Haiku*, "Now Wild Geese Return," Op. 50, No. 12
© 1963 Theodore Presser Company. Used by permission of the publisher.

Piano, Four Hands

Pianists frequently must glance away from their music to see the conductor, to see other members of the ensemble, to give cues, and so on. In Chapter 1, a reference was made to "an invisible, elastic tether" pulling your eyes back to the exact point on the page at which you are playing. The duet exercises that follow (Figures 3.17 and 3.18) are designed to assist in the development of that technique.

Practicing these exercises is a little like watching a tennis match on television. One is able to follow the back-and-forth motion of the ball without turning the head from side to side. When the ball hits the court, but before it is returned, the eyes can anticipate the return and move to the opposite court. While this does not allow one to study the form of the players, it does involve the spectator in other strategies of the game. That technique is similar to the one required in executing the following exercises.

The piano duets are to be played by one person. The left hand will play from the *secondo* page while the right hand will play from the *primo* page. It is crucial to not move the head from side to side but, rather, to allow the eyes to sweep from page to page. Before practicing Figure 3.17 at the piano, prepare by silent study:

Secondo

FIGURE 3.17   Daniel G. Türk, *Chorale*

1. At ♩ = 66, first let your eyes move rhythmically from page to page, reading half note by half note (left hand on bass line of *secondo* page and right hand on melody of *primo* page).

2. When this feels somewhat comfortable, play.

3. Once you are comfortable playing, change from ♩ = 66 to 𝅗𝅥 = 33. Then gradually increase tempo to ♩ = 88 and 𝅗𝅥 = 44.

4. Once you are comfortable playing one line in each hand, you may increase the difficulty by playing all of the *primo* page in the right hand against the bass line of the *secondo* part, working carefully through the previous tempos. As the level of difficulty increases, be sure to keep the purpose of the exercise in mind: continuous and rhythmic movement of the eyes. It is also an exercise in playing from recall.

5. The *secondo* page can be played in its entirety with the left hand by transposing the bass line up one octave.

The only necessary parts of the exercise are 1 and 2. If 3, 4, and 5 are overly taxing, simply omit them and return to them later.

Primo

Figure 3.18 is a duet with a more horizontal texture than that found in Figure 3.17. As a result, the eyes will now move from note to note. Otherwise, the basic reason for the exercise is the same as before: The eyes must move rhythmically and continuously from page to page while you play from recall. The approach

FIGURE 3.18   Heinrich Wohlfahrt, *Bagatelle*

to this duet may be somewhat less rigid than in the *Chorale*. One will be generally free to mix and match more imaginatively; for example, the left hand may play the upper *secondo* line throughout, or the right hand may play the lower *primo* part.

Scores

Score reading is one of the ultimate tests of flowing visual activity because it thoroughly combines vertical scanning, recall, and side-to-side scanning.

Practice Figure 3.19 as follows:

Measures 1–16:   1st violin and cello ($\quad$ = 72–84)

     17–24:   flute and 1st violin ($\quad$ = 72–84)

     25–32:   flute and 2nd violin ($\quad$ = 58–72)

     25–32:   flute and 1st violin in octaves against 2nd violin in left hand ($\quad$ = 63–72)

     32–46:   oboes against 2nd violin ($\quad$ = 63)

To encourage playing from recall and looking ahead, ask someone to cover the measure being played on or by the second beat.

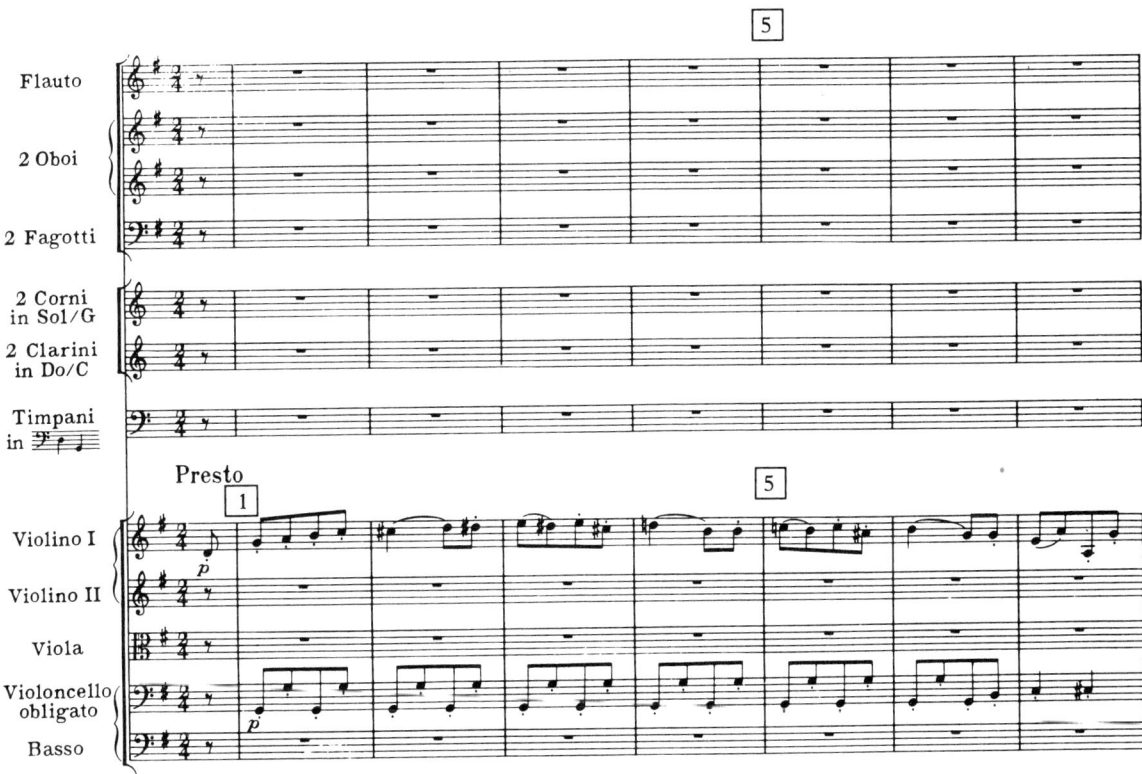

FIGURE 3.19   Franz Joseph Haydn, *Symphony No. 92*, Presto

FIGURE 3.19, continued

(continued)

FIGURE 3.19, continued

FIGURE 3.19, continued

The Bach fugue in Figure 3.20 is an arrangement from *The Well-Tempered Clavier*, originally for a soloist. In this scored form, the individual voice movement is easier to discern. The reason for presenting this example now should become clear as you read the instructions for playing it.

The goal is to play the entire fugue as a trio, without stopping at any time to regroup. During the course of the fugue, someone will surely become lost. At that time, his or her job will be to ascertain where the others are, through scanning the other parts, and to be able to reenter.

1. Assign one player to a part.

2. Turn on a metronome.

3. Begin.

If total breakdown does occur, begin again, with the addition of a conductor, who will call out measure numbers and beats when confusion arises. The rhythm will continue in any case. Measures and beats will be called until the group is playing together again.

Try a third time, without a conductor but with everyone counting aloud. If someone gets lost, he or she should scan the various parts to become reoriented.

FIGURE 3.20 J. S. Bach, *The Well-Tempered Clavier*, Fuga XXI
Reprinted by permission of Belwin-Mills Publishing
Company c/o CPP/Belwin, Inc., Miami, FL 33014.

FIGURE 3.20, continued

(continued)

FIGURE 3.20, continued

CHAPTER FOUR

Contact

Sight-reading instruction rarely includes attention to fingerings; nevertheless, they are as important in reading as in performing rehearsed music. Sluggish, inert hands and fingers that remain in place are a primary hindrance to competent reading. Flexible, supple fingerings choreograph the hands for maximum efficiency of the fingers and are a principal means to acquiring manual agility. They are the only way for the hands to maintain contact with the keyboard; without that contact, reading improves slowly, if at all.

Looking down at the keyboard—the sure sign of a weak reader—occurs because contact is lost. Looking down is the end of a chain reaction. The reader, through lack of coordination or having run short of fingers, lifts his or her hands from the keyboard. The reader must then look down, because the hands are suspended in the air and cannot feel what follows. Looking down is an unacceptable way to determine what note comes next.

The only other, reliable way to sense and locate the next note(s) is to be able to maintain the feel of what you have just played; then you can determine the following intervals. Only through active fingerings can the hand maintain constant feel of the keyboard. Astute fingerings are essential for correct perception of horizontal intervals.

Most piano students have spent considerable time practicing technical exercises, including scales, arpeggios, chord progressions, and etudes; yet, their reading often lags far behind their acquired fluency. Many have developed the notion that fingers must always be used consecutively. Adept pianists frequently utilize noncontiguous fingerings, because consecutive fingers simply are not always available. Substitutions, unorthodox crossings, and slides position the hands to provide those "extra fingers" and to find escape routes.

Understanding these concepts of fingerings will require some time. Practicing them, however, should involve as little rote work as possible—only enough to technically establish the principle. Avoid becoming mired in repetitions that block spontaneity.

A well-defined legato builds musical as well as technical independence, making possible the sorting of musical lines. Once you have developed the sense of harmonic reading and have learned to feel and sense the logic of fingering, you can better project musical layers, direction, and an understanding of the page on first playing.

Because legato touch is central to modern organ technique, an organist's fingers are in almost constant contact with the keyboard. Many of the following exercises are borrowed from organ sources. You should practice all the exercises without using the damper pedal, to learn the feeling of contact from the hands rather than depending on the pedal to help produce connected sound.

In general, become aware of what the fingers are doing. The hand will learn how to balance on any one of them. Then the fingers can have some fun.

SUBSTITUTION

Practice Figures 4.1 through 4.4.

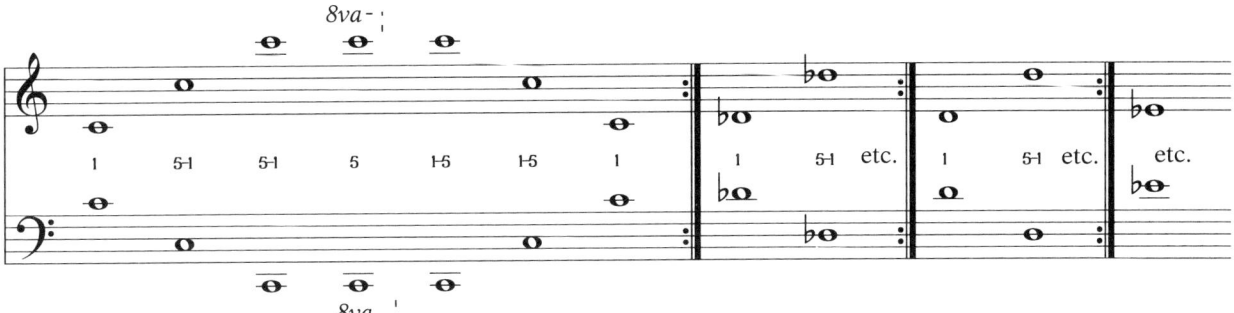

FIGURE 4.1

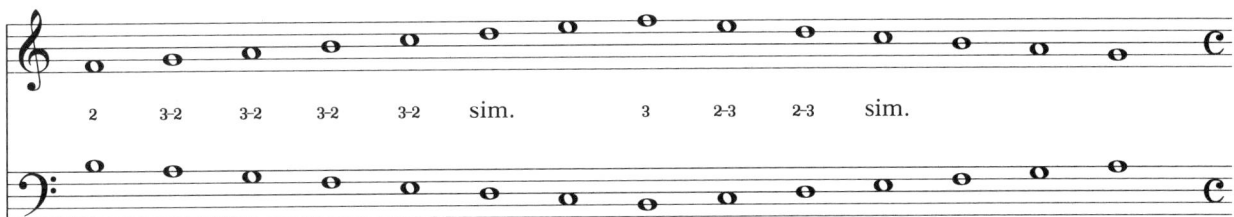

FIGURE 4.2

Practice Figure 4.2 also with alternative combinations, such as:

1 3-1 3-1 3-1 . . .

1 4-1 4-1 4-1 . . .

3 5-3 5-3 5-3 . . .

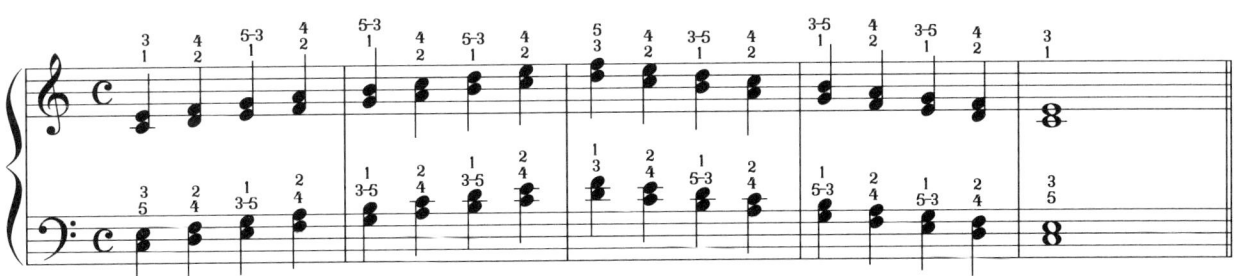

FIGURE 4.3   Edward Shippen Barnes, from *School of Organ Playing*, Op. 31
Published by The Boston Music Co., 116 Boylston St.,
Boston, Ma. 02116 and used by permission.

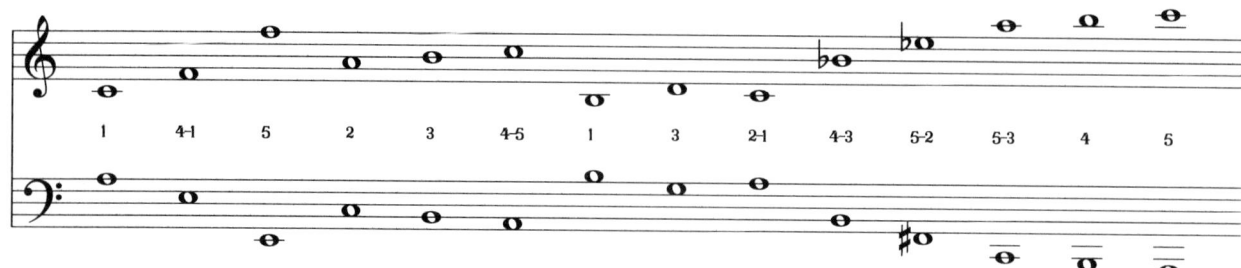

FIGURE 4.4

Practice Figure 4.4 also with your eyes closed as a friend calls intervals and fingerings. Feel the interval before you play the next note. Play several times, starting on a different note each time.

The short phrase in Figure 4.5 is repeated in Figures 4.6 and 4.7 with typically unstudied and amateur fingerings. Obvious shortcomings include loss of contact and poor voice-leading. The pianist probably sees the music only vertically, not horizontally, and sees it only one beat at a time.

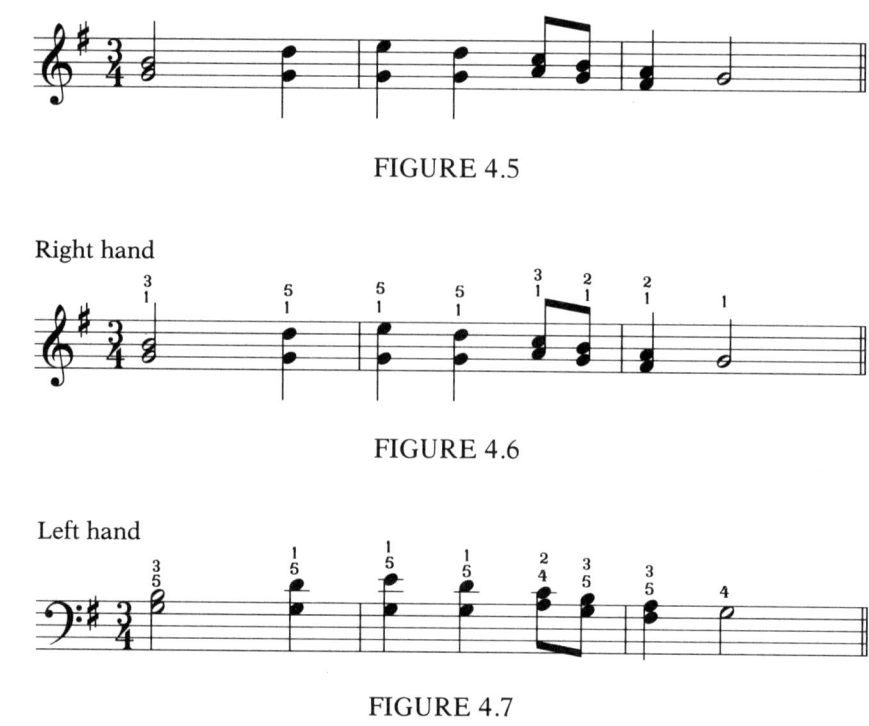

FIGURE 4.5

Right hand

FIGURE 4.6

Left hand

FIGURE 4.7

The following four versions of the exercise suggest how substitutions improve contact, legato, and horizontal reading.

1. Figure 4.8 shows the exercise as a pianist sees it.

FIGURE 4.8

SUBSTITUTION
53

2. Figure 4.9 shows the exercise as a pianist understands and executes it.

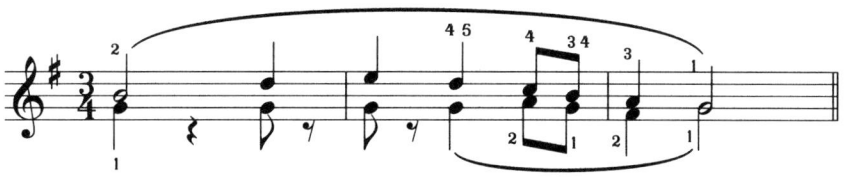

FIGURE 4.9

3. Figure 4.10 shows the exercise in score form for easier reading.

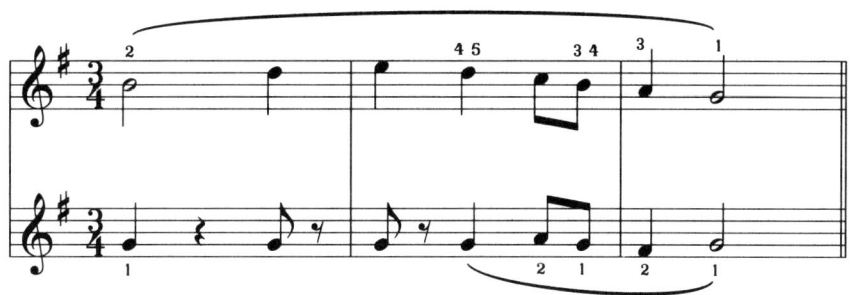

FIGURE 4.10

4. Figure 4.11 shows the exercise as written for left hand. Apply the same manner of releases and substitutions as described for the right hand.

FIGURE 4.11

Care is given to substitution for several reasons: (1) to position the hand so that it may find exits and make more fingers available, (2) to maintain contact with the keyboard, and (3) to promote more sensible voice-leading.

SLIDES

It is permissible and sometimes advisable to slide from one note to another. This technique is especially useful when moving from black notes to white notes. At times, it will rescue a player from a tight spot that has occurred through a miscalculation or a simple error. At other times, it can be planned into a fingering pattern as one of the more desirable fingerings. This technique is applied in some passages from Beethoven sonatas, for instance, particularly as fingered by Artur Schnabel.

Slides are most often done from black note to white note, with either hand, using any finger. They should be practiced without pedal and with no loss of contact or sound between sliding finger and keyboard.

A slide from white note to white note is most often done with the thumb and more closely resembles a creeping motion than an actual slide. To move with the right hand from B to C, for example, play C with the thumb tip. Then move from thumb tip on the key to the first thumb joint on the key to sustain the tone. Turn the thumb tip outward toward B. There will be three movements on each note played. Do all three as smoothly as possible (Figures 4.12 through 4.14).

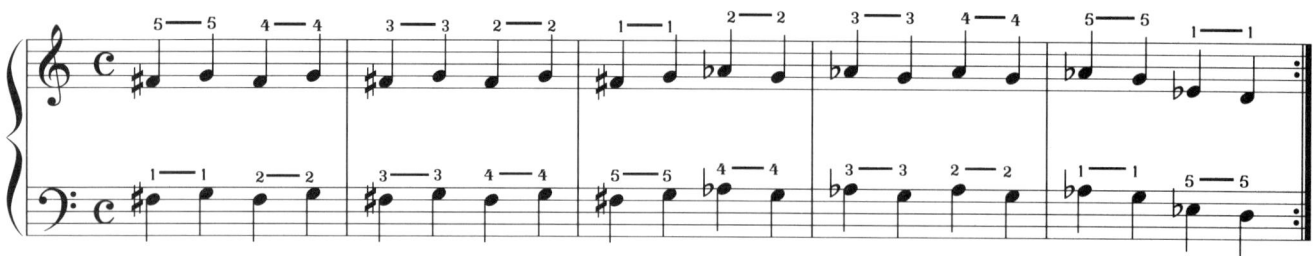

FIGURE 4.12   Edward Shippen Barnes, from *School of Organ Playing*, Op. 31
Published by The Boston Music Co., 116 Boylston St.,
Boston, Ma. 02116 and used by permission.

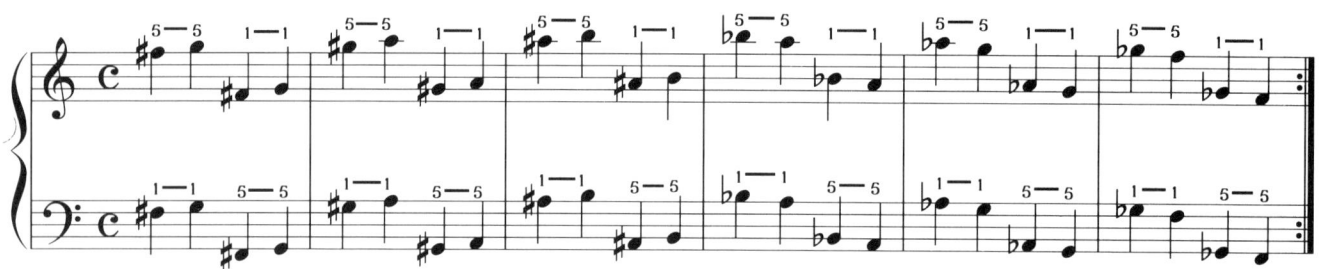

FIGURE 4.13   Edward Shippen Barnes, from *School of Organ Playing*, Op. 31
Published by The Boston Music Co., 116 Boylston St.,
Boston, Ma. 02116 and used by permission.

FIGURE 4.14   Edward Shippen Barnes, from *School of Organ Playing*, Op. 31
Published by The Boston Music Co., 116 Boylston St.,
Boston, Ma. 02116 and used by permission.

UNORTHODOX CROSSINGS

Practice Figure 4.15 with alternative fingerings, such as 424242, 323232, and 535353.

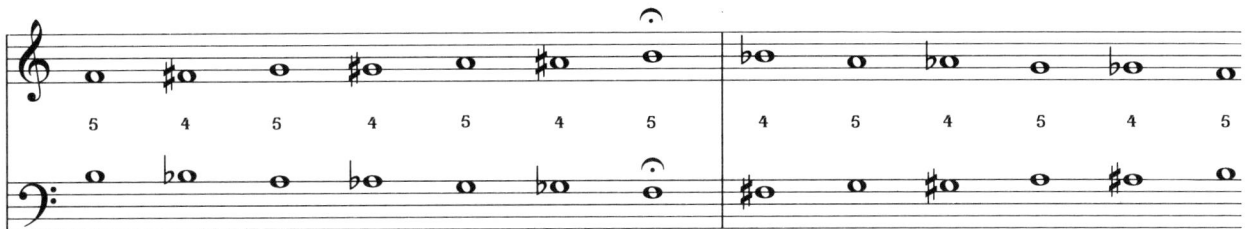

FIGURE 4.15

Practice Figure 4.16 with other fingering combinations, such as 523523, 134134, and 124124.

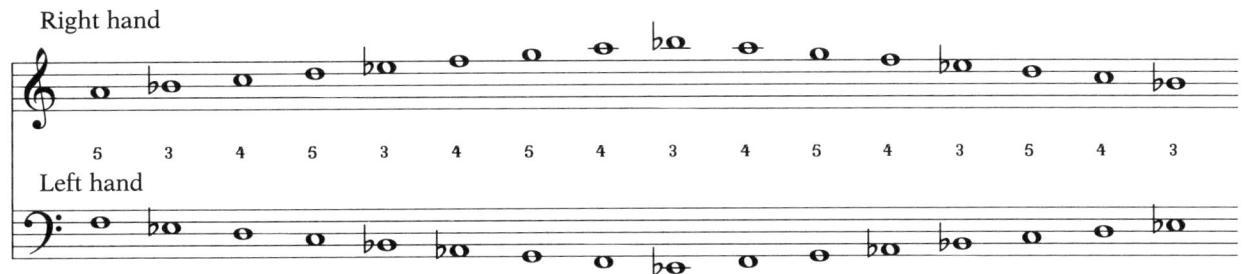

FIGURE 4.16

Practice Figure 4.17 using the given fingerings.

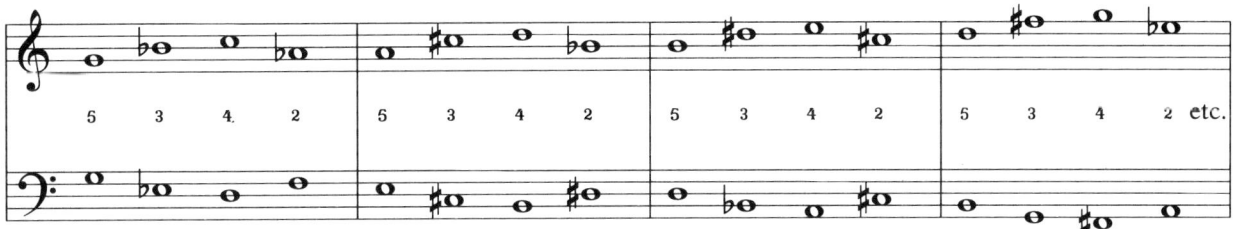

FIGURE 4.17

Play Figure 4.18 as slowly as necessary (♪ = 46), giving adequate time to plan. While still holding the notes you have just played, feel within your hand the next notes and fingerings. The progression must be steady and regular throughout the exercise. Also practice with outermost lines legato against staccato inner lines.

FIGURE 4.18   Exercise by Rudolph Ganz

Practice Figure 4.19 as written, increasing the tempo to ♩ = 116. If your hands are small and have difficulty reaching octaves and ninths, adapt the exercise, possibly repeating measures 1–3 several times.

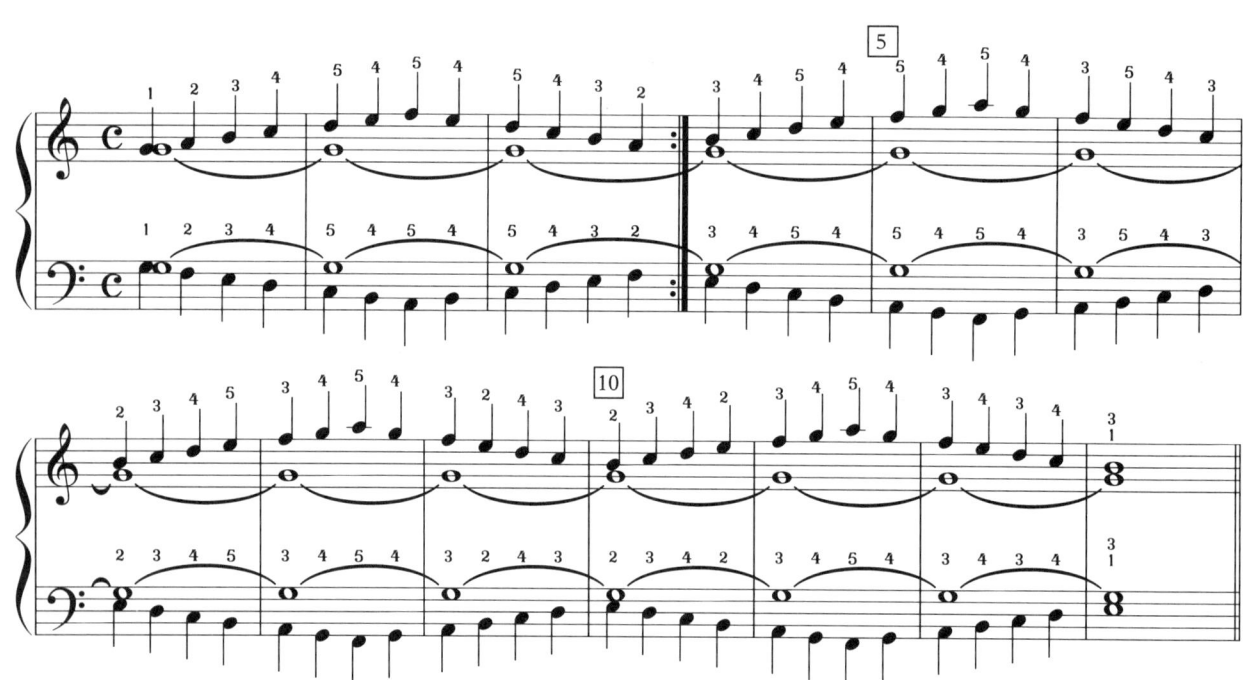

FIGURE 4.19   Edward Shippen Barnes, from *School of Organ Playing*, Op. 31
Published by The Boston Music Co., 116 Boylston St.,
Boston, Ma. 02116 and used by permission.

BALANCED INDEPENDENCE

As implied in preceding fingering exercises, sustaining a note is the ultimate keyboard contact and should be achieved through any means possible, as long as the musical sensibility is maintained. It is often possible to sustain only one note while the rest of a chord must be released to facilitate the next move. To achieve this, the fingers require independence from one another so that the hand can balance on any one finger as the others organize the next move. This skill is frequently overlooked in piano playing even at advanced levels, but it is essential to gaining an intuitive sense of the keyboard at any time and to achieving beautiful legato.

The exercises in Figures 4.20 through 4.27 develop skill in balanced independence while continuing to limber up the hand through substitutions and unorthodox crossings. Connect each whole note to the next in an absolutely legato manner while you play the other notes, as indicated, very staccato. It is important to train the ear as well as the hand to perceive this difference in articulation, so that old habits will not reassert themselves.

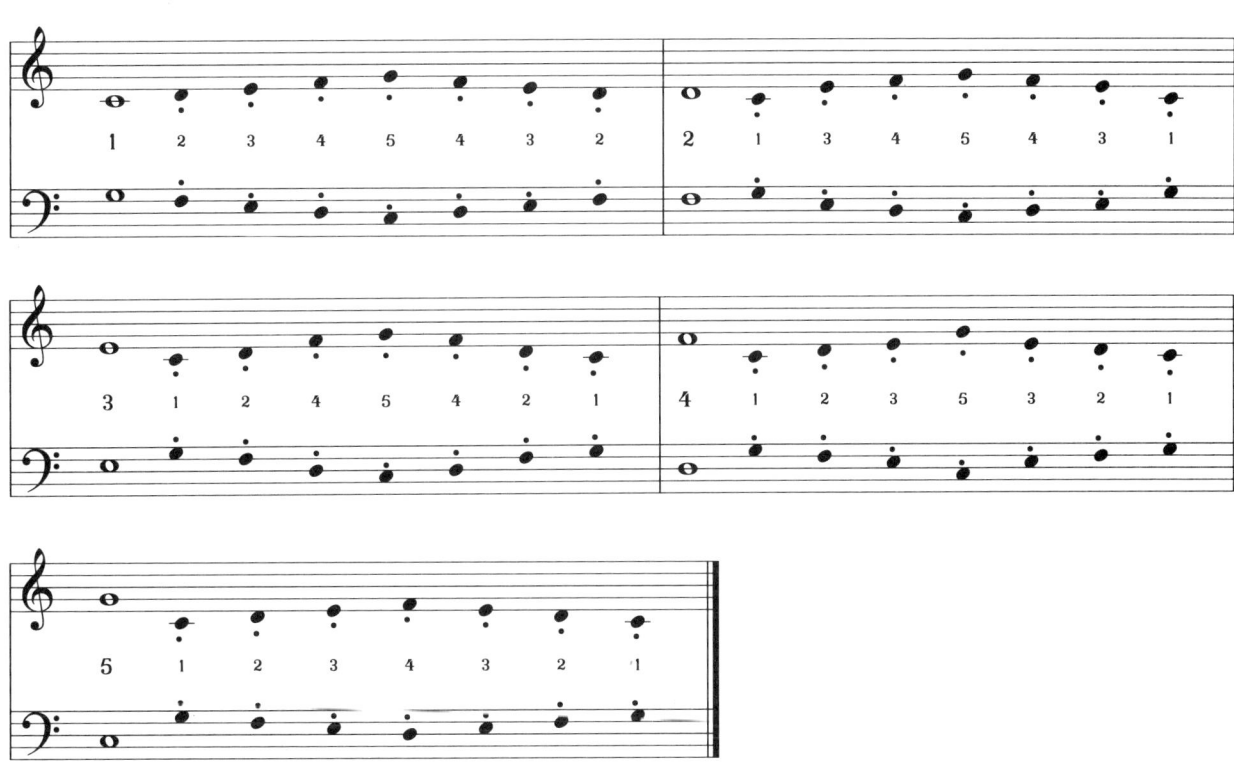

FIGURE 4.20

FIGURE 4.21

In Figures 4.22 and 4.23, release all black notes. Connect each white note to the next white note.

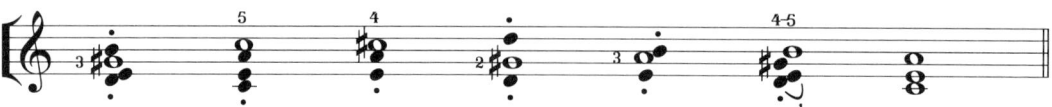

FIGURE 4.22

Left hand

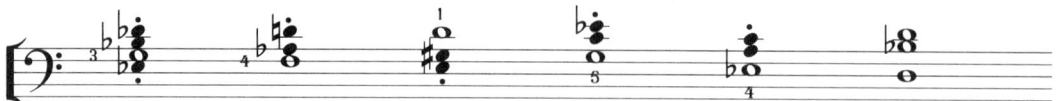

FIGURE 4.23

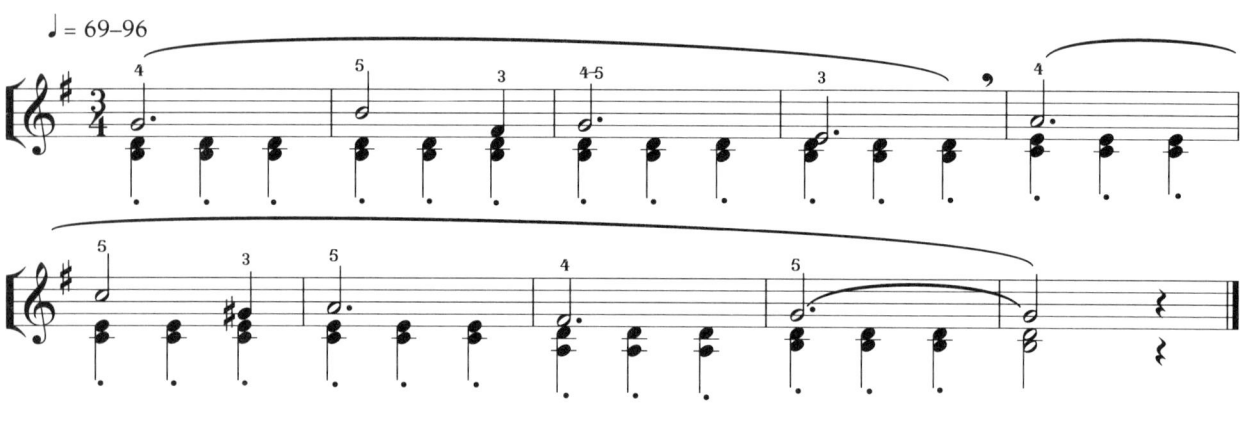

FIGURE 4.24

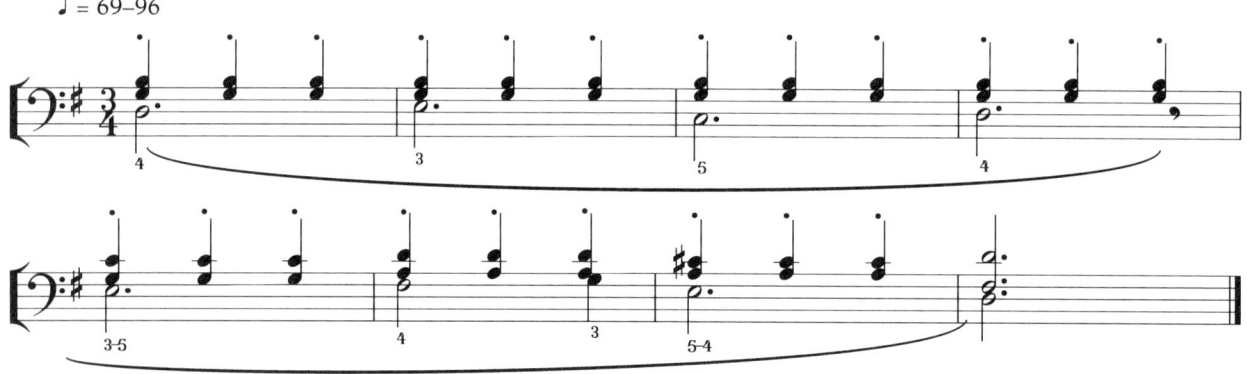

FIGURE 4.25

FIGURE 4.26

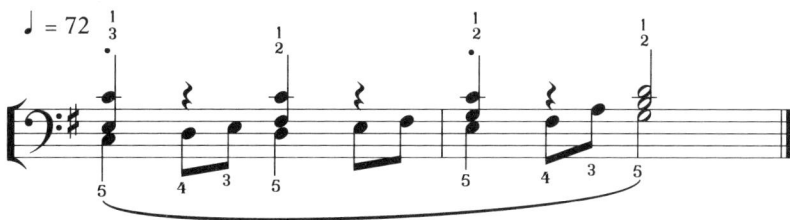

FIGURE 4.27

The next three musical examples incorporate releases and sustained melodic tones in the same hand.

Figure 4.28 is an excerpt from the slow movement of a Weber piano sonata. Play it as written.

FIGURE 4.28   Carl Maria von Weber, *Sonata No. 2*, Andante

In Figure 4.29, notice that most chord tones lie above the melody.

1. The right hand plays the upper three lines. (In measure 7, the fourth beat is best played by the left hand, as indicated.)

2. The left hand plays only the lowest single line (omit if preferred).

FIGURE 4.29   Dvořák-Labuta, *Symphony No. 9*, Finale
Reprinted from Joseph A. Labuta, *Basic Conducting Techniques*, copyright © 1982 by Prentice-Hall.

Figure 4.30 is from a Chopin nocturne. Play it as written. Work in two-measure fragments, hands alone, then hands together.

FIGURE 4.30   Frédéric Chopin, *Nocturne*, Op. 15, No. 3

Figure 4.31 is to be practiced as an etude, using the following procedures:

1. Tie those notes that do not change between chords. Notice the lengthy stretches (measures 3–5 and 8–12, for example) where no voice moves—all of these will be tied. The tempo should be ♩ = 66–100.

2. Play, striking all tones as written but with the moving voice always perfectly legato. Use tempo ♩ = 66–100.

3. Play stylistically with proper articulation, but continue to feel the next note-change before striking it. The tempo should be ♩ = 92–112.

FIGURE 4.31   Bela Bartók, from *Mikrokosmos*,
Book V, "Chords Together and Opposed"
Copyright © by Boosey & Hawkes.

An exercise earlier used for legato in the upper line is now presented for a different purpose. In Figure 4.32, attention is paid to the alto line, which, until the middle of measure 2, is continuously broken. Notice the rhythmic release of the repeated alto notes, shown by the rests. Without this rhythmic release, the thumb will sustain its note until the last split second, causing the entire hand to be involuntarily pulled off the keyboard. When it is necessary to release a note, do so systematically, releasing half its value.

FIGURE 4.32

Hidden Repeated Notes

Figure 4.33 contains four types of repeated notes that require systematic releases. A, B, and C have been covered in previous exercises. D, hidden repeated notes, is new.

A. The notes are repeated either in one voice or in two voices at once, either hand.
   1. Left hand: measures 1–2, 3
   2. Right hand: measures 1, 5, 6, 9, 11, 13, 14, 15

B. There is a double line within one hand—one voice legato, the other repeated.
   1. Left hand, tenor: measures 5–7 and 9–12
   2. Right hand, alto: measure 13

C. The note doesn't repeat, but the thumb or finger(s) must move.
   1. Right hand: measures 2–3

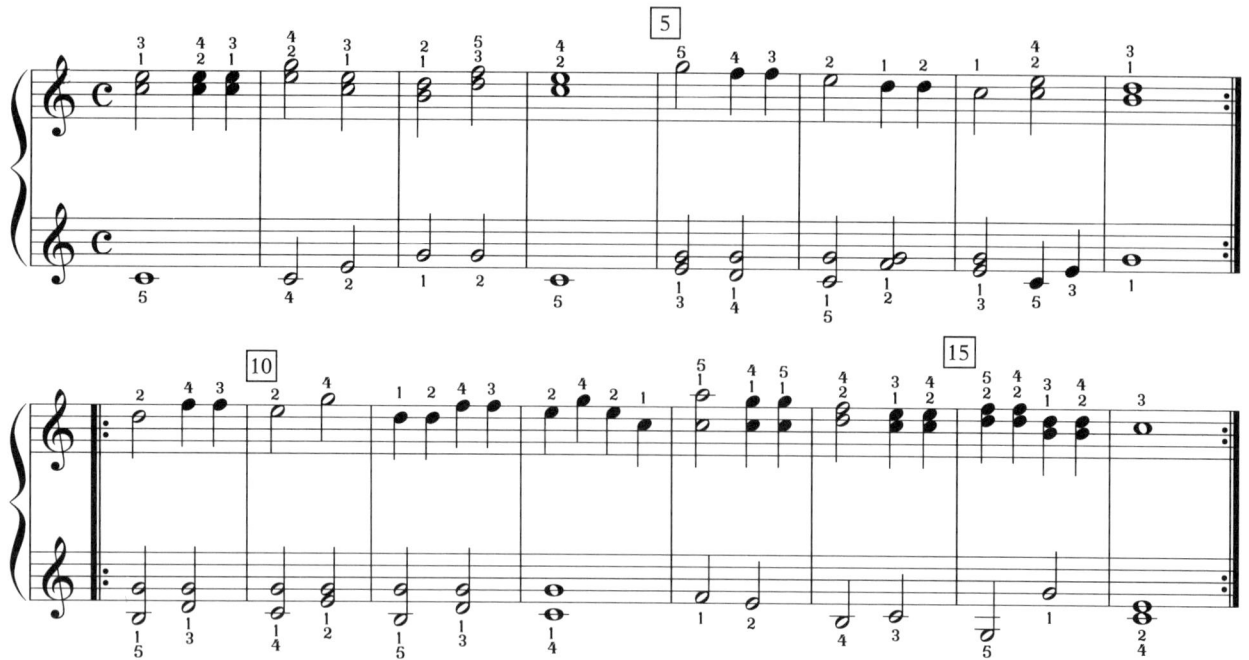

FIGURE 4.33 Carl Czerny, *Trio*, from Opus 453

D. *Hidden repeated notes:* This occurs when a note crosses voices. All examples are in the right hand.
 1. Measures 1–2: Soprano E becomes alto E.
 2. Measure 2: Alto E returns to soprano E.
 3. Measure 3: Soprano D becomes alto D.
 4. Measure 15: Alto D becomes soprano D.

The next two excerpts clarify D. Figure 4.34 shows the repetitions in question. Figure 4.35 encircles only the finger that must release.

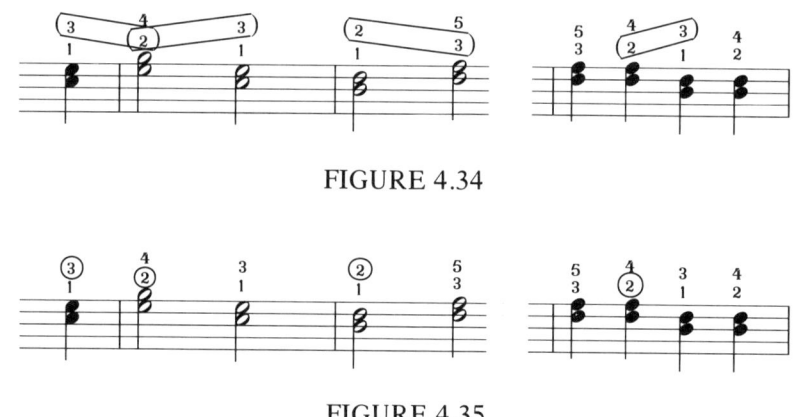

FIGURE 4.34

FIGURE 4.35

In Figure 4.36, first practice the repetitions with a systematic release, as in this edited example. At no time is there to be a complete break; at least one voice must be in contact with the keyboard at all times (except when both voices repeat, as in the right hand, measure 1). Then practice trying the repeated tones.

FIGURE 4.36 Carl Czerny, *Trio*, from Opus 453

Practice also from the unedited example (Figure 4.37) to identify for yourself the occurrences of systematic releases.

FIGURE 4.37 Carl Czerny, *Trio*, from Opus 453

Total contact will appear by increments. The trio bristles with releases, and you should understand that you will miss quite a few the first time. Expect yourself to include more releases in each successive encounter.

First reading—30% accurate releases

Second reading—50% accurate releases

Third reading—85% accurate releases

Then return at a later time, expecting yet a higher percentage of accuracy.

Continue practicing the systematic release of repeated notes or of notes that cannot be connected while maintaining absolute connections where possible. In Figure 4.38, use one color of pencil to mark broken voices and another color to denote connections where most or all other voices break.

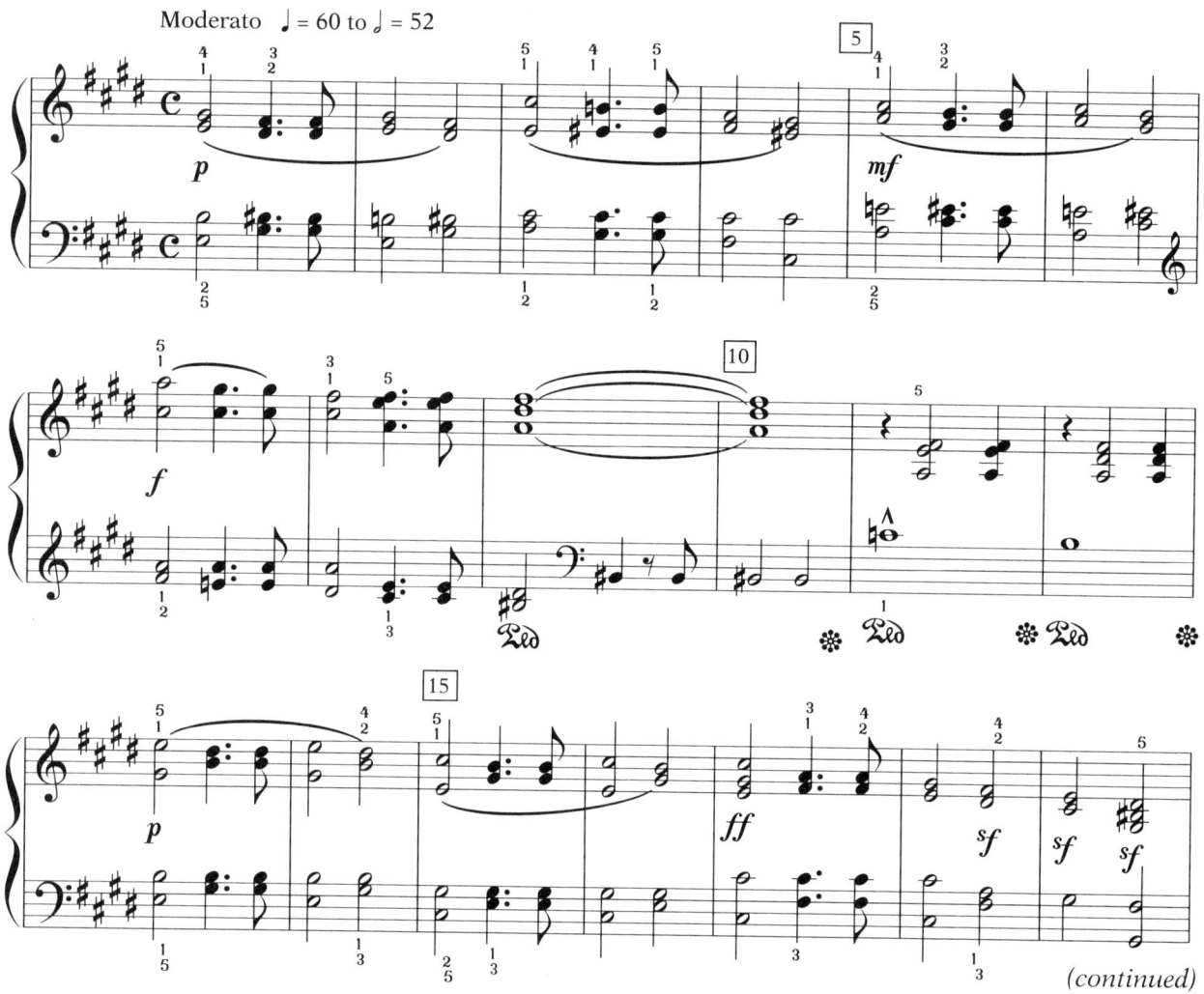

FIGURE 4.38 Stephen Heller, *Moderato*

FIGURE 4.38, continued

Figures 4.39 and 4.40, from the piano repertoire, have examples of the kinds of fingering we have discussed. Practice these exercises to experience the balance and agility such fingerings make possible.

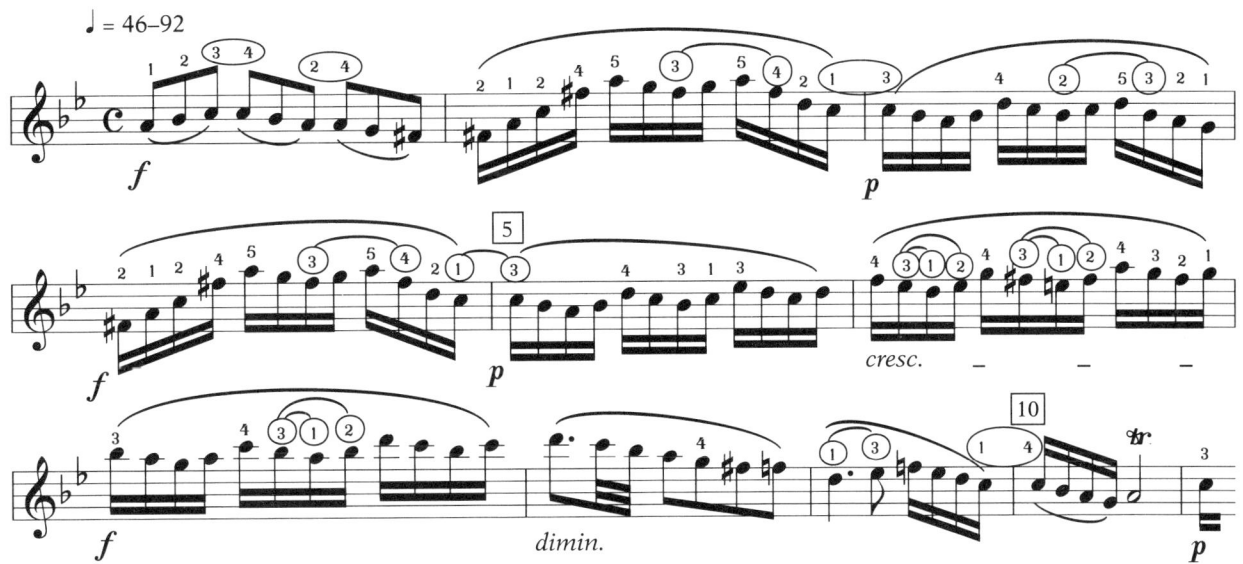

FIGURE 4.39   Muzio Clementi, *Sonatina*, Op. 38, No. 2

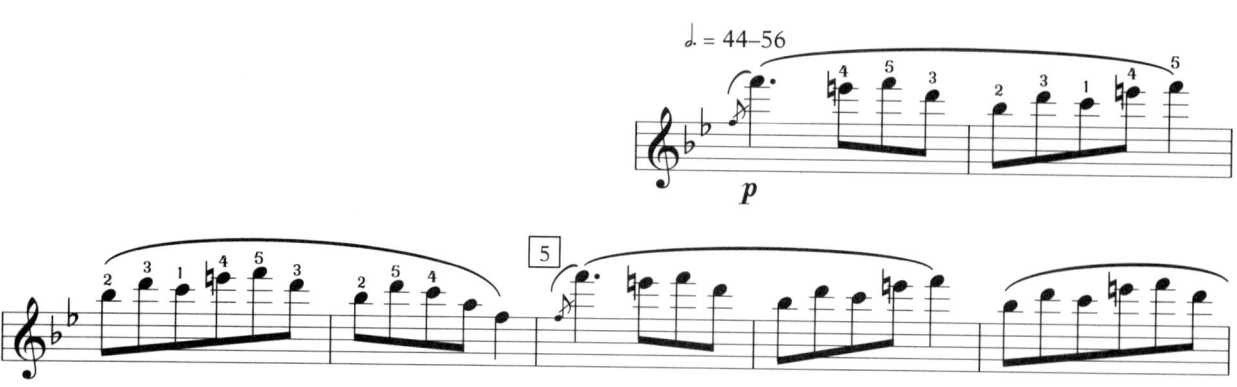

FIGURE 4.40   Frédéric Chopin, *Mazurka*, Op. 68, No. 3
Reprinted from Frédéric Chopin *Mazurkas*. Published by PWM Edition.

Figure 4.41 is riddled with fingering schemes that maintain good horizontal lines. It contains examples of silent substitutions, repeated-note substitutions, noncontiguous fingerings, fingers that cross over or under each other, and so on.

In each voice, find and circle every example of such fingerings. The soprano line should have about sixteen such examples, the bass lines about nine, and the alto line about four.

Practice the individual lines until the fingerings seem easy. Do not look down at the keyboard—instead, feel the interval.

(continued)

FIGURE 4.41   J. S. Bach, *Little Prelude in C*
Kleine Präludien und Fughetten, No. 5, edited by Steglich and Theopold,
copyright 1987 by G. Henle, München. Reprinted by permission.

FIGURE 4.41, continued

In Figure 4.42, the accompaniment combines elements of many of the preceding exercises. Finger it for right-hand legato and for constant contact in each hand, and redistribute the inner voice so that it flows continuously (for example, measure 5, third finger, left hand).

Play the edited accompaniment with a soloist as a check for agility and suitability of fingerings.

Exchange completed assignments, so that each student plays from another's fingerings.

FIGURE 4.42 Henry Purcell, *King Arthur*,
"Fairest Isle"; words by John Dryden

(continued)

FIGURE 4.42, continued

The following three exercises are a condensation of the piece "Bells," which follows (Figure 4.46). Once you have reviewed the exercises, read the piece. While reading, be sure to maintain soft eyes and let your eyes sweep from measure to measure.

Figure 4.43 corresponds to measures 4–12. Work out fingering so that each hand maintains contact with the keyboard between every chord.

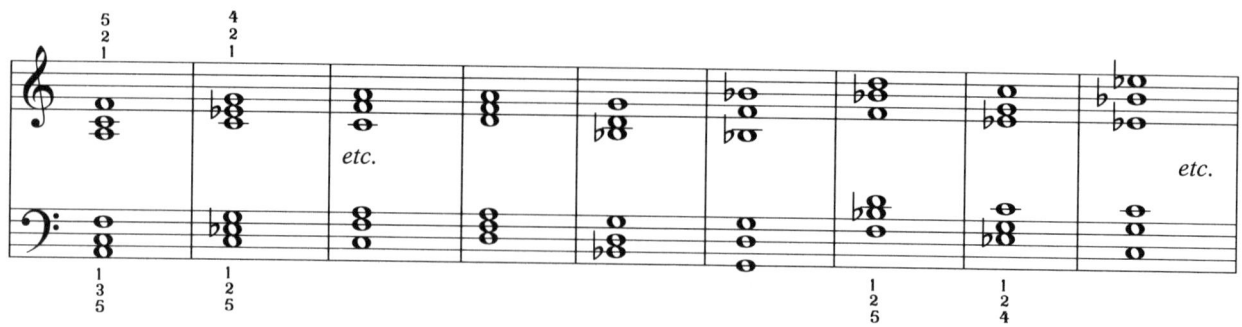

FIGURE 4.43

Figure 4.44 corresponds to measures 31–34. Finger so that you can play the phrase accurately and reliably without looking at the keyboard.

FIGURE 4.44

Figure 4.45 corresponds to measures 26–29 and 35–44. This is not a fingering exercise—use $\frac{5}{4}$ with a loose wrist. Pedal throughout each measure.

1

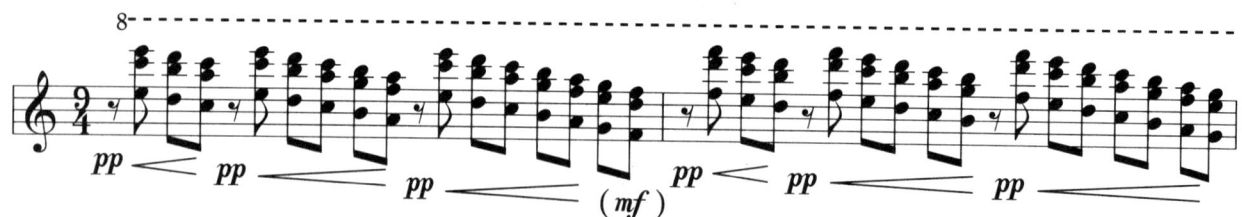

FIGURE 4.45

FIGURE 4.46   Peter Arnstein, *Bells*
Reprinted from *Piano Compositions Emphasizing Large
Physical Movement*, copyright © 1989 by Peter Arnstein.

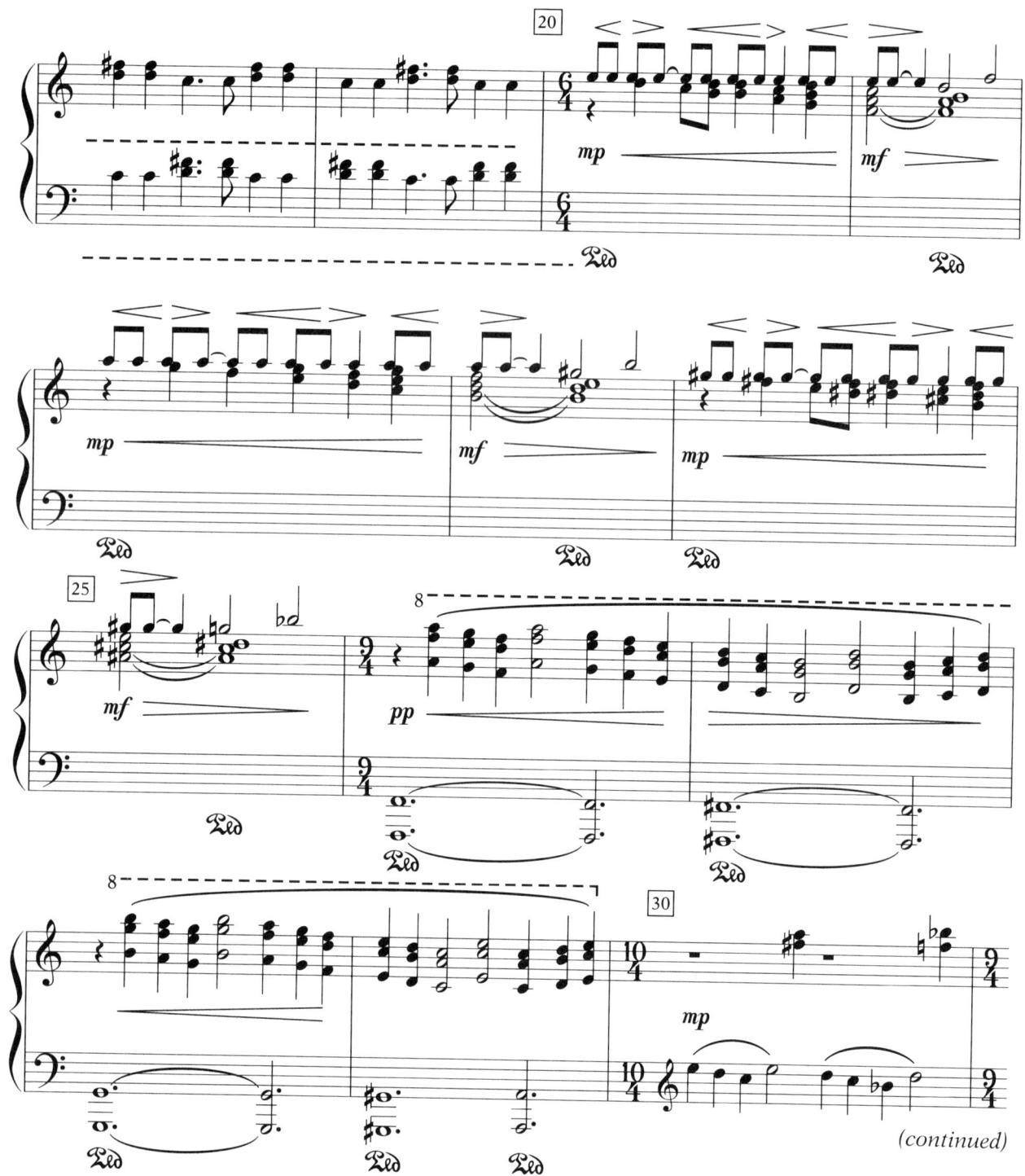

FIGURE 4.46, continued

FIGURE 4.46, continued

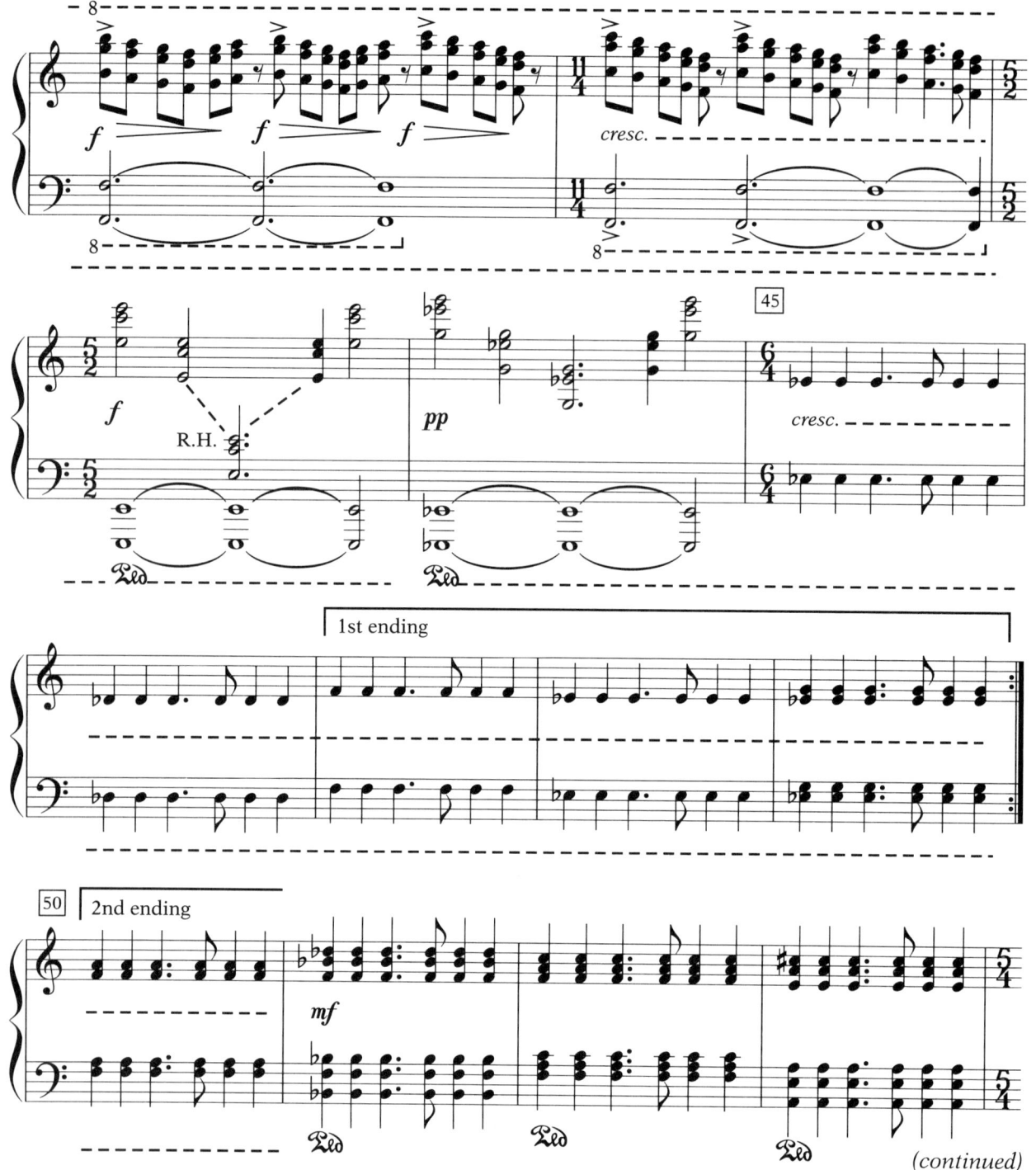

FIGURE 4.46, continued

FIGURE 4.46, continued

LEAPS

Play-Move-Place

As the preceding exercises and examples have shown, it is important to maintain contact with the keyboard whenever possible; however, piano music abounds with leaps and reaches that make continuous contact impossible. It is essential at such times to *be on the note before it is time to play the note*. The release of a note or a chord should feel nearly simultaneous with moving to the next location. Failure contributes to looking down and interrupted rhythm.

To describe the technique of leaps, we can use a three-part procedure called *play-move-place*. These introductory exercises are a condensation of that procedure.

In Figure 4.47, each part of *play-move-place* receives one beat.

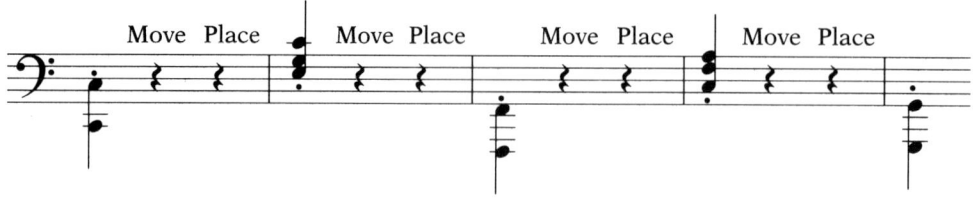

FIGURE 4.47

Figure 4.48 condenses *play* and *move* into one beat.

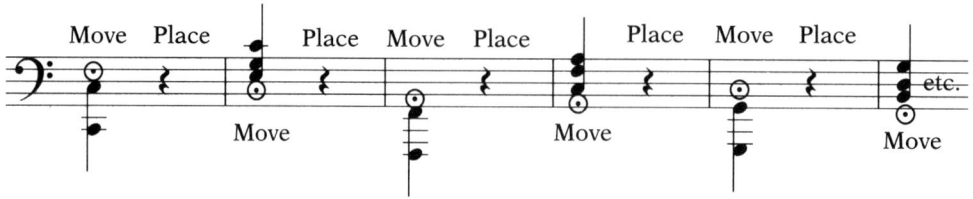

FIGURE 4.48

In Figure 4.49, *play, move,* and *place* occur simultaneously. Be on the new chord or octave at X.

FIGURE 4.49

The next excerpt you will play is from Rebikov's *Dance of the Little Ones* (Figure 4.58). The sight-reading drill for the excerpt is as follows:

1. The right hand has no need to move; it covers a five-note, whole-tone scale (Figure 4.50).

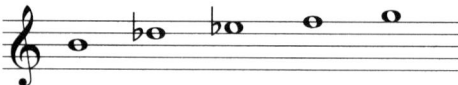

FIGURE 4.50

2. The left hand is divided into two parts:
   a. E♭ octave drone (Figure 4.51)

FIGURE 4.51

b. Parallel minor sixths in paired groups (Figure 4.52)

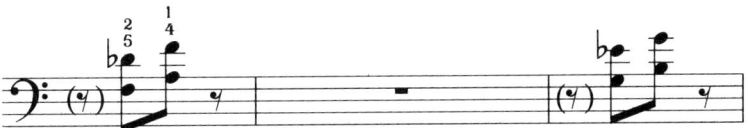

FIGURE 4.52

3. The drone and the sixths are connected by left-hand jumps.
    a. The distance from the octave drone *up* to the sixths can be measured from the top finger of the octave (1) to the lower finger of the sixth (5) (Figure 4.53). The distance can also be measured from the thumb of the octave to the second finger of the sixth (Figure 4.54).

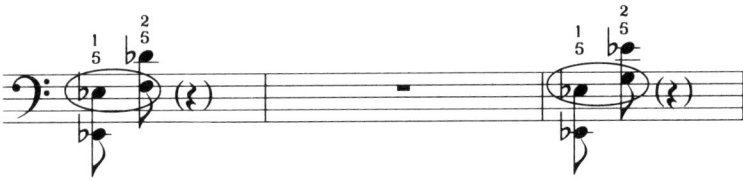

FIGURE 4.53

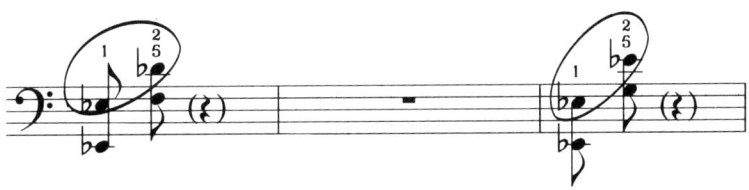

FIGURE 4.54

    b. The distance from the sixth *down* to the next octave can be measured from the low note of the sixth (4) to the top note of the octave (1) (Figure 4.55). It can also be measured from thumb to thumb (Figure 4.56).

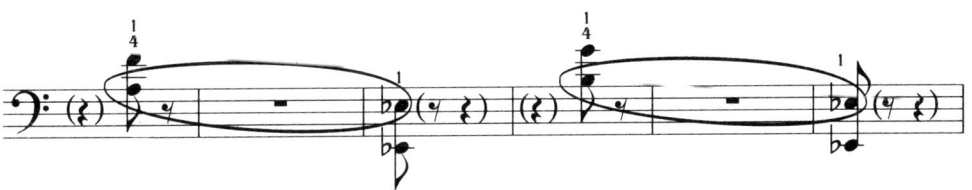

FIGURE 4.55

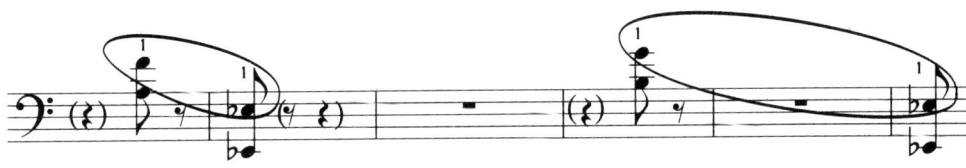

FIGURE 4.56

4. When playing the total bass line, the left hand should *place* the new octave by the downbeat of the silent measure (Figure 4.57).

FIGURE 4.57

Play-move-place should be practiced until it is a basic part of your body's rhythmic perception of music. This response must become immediate. It will assist the so-called reading ahead. The *move-place* movement must be practiced *without* looking at the keyboard. Practice such fragments with eyes closed.

Figure 4.58 is a section of the original piece from which the preceding examples were drawn. Practice the excerpt, trying to apply those principles discussed in the exercises.

FIGURE 4.58   Vladimir Rebikov, from *Dance of the Little Ones*, Op. 35, No. 6
© 1983 Theodore Presser Company.

Figure 4.59 gives additional practice in left hand leaps. Remember that the left hand should be on its next notes by the last half of beats one and two.

FIGURE 4.59   César Franck, from *Langsamer Tanz* ("Slow Dance")

In Figure 4.60, *play-move-place* occurs relentlessly in both hands throughout the accompaniment. Practice measures 1–12 until the procedure feels secure; then proceed through the song adding four-measure increments. Finally, try speaking or singing the vocal line while playing the accompaniment.

FIGURE 4.60   Jules Massenet, from *October Roses*

FIGURE 4.60, continued

And why_____ days so quick - ly glow - ing?
Pour - quoi_____ ces bré - ves tour - né - es?

FIGURE 4.60, continued

PLAY-MOVE-PLACE LEGATO

Even when the music contains no leaps whatsoever and when one has attained a fine legato through the most connected fingerings possible, the *play-place* idea applies. While the pianist is connecting one chord with all or some notes sustained, three things are happening within the hand:

1. It is sensing the location of the new chord.

2. It is feeling the horizontal intervals between the old and the new chords.

3. It is feeling the shape of the new chord.

All of that occurs simultaneously. The sensation is quite physical for the player, although it is invisible to the observer. If it is happening, it can be heard musically in a smooth and contoured line. If it is not happening, the musical effect will be choppy and incontinuous. If at all possible, one should always be on or sense the note(s) before it is time to play the note(s).

In Figure 4.61, do the following:

1. Play the first chord and hold it while scanning the entire exercise. Your hand should sense an internal tug in the direction of every chord you read.

2. Play in slow half notes, ♩ = 72. You will feel the new chord on beat 2 while holding the old chord.

3. Play in quick half notes, ♩ = 88, so that the old chord and the new chord are felt almost simultaneously. The hand will have the sensation of continuous gliding.

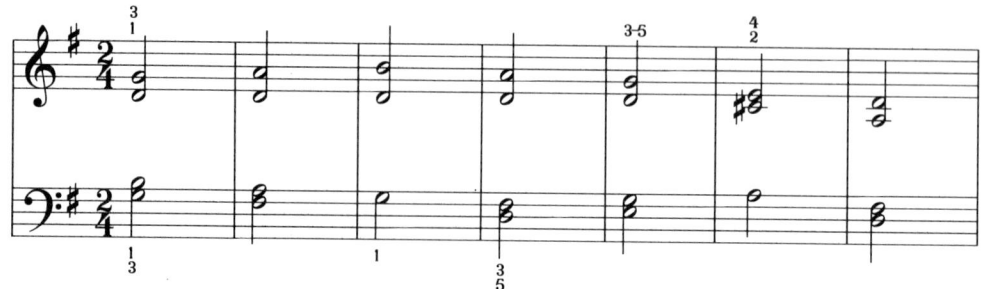

FIGURE 4.61

CHAPTER FIVE

Horizontal Intervals

HORIZONTAL READING

It is important that the hand feel the keyboard distance of an interval it is about to play. Without this feel, the pianist is forced to look at the keyboard to spot the next note. The pianist's feel of the interval before playing it parallels a singer's hearing an interval before singing it.

Figure 5.1 must not be seen as two separate events but as a distance. Figure 5.2 must not be seen as two separate notes but as a perfect fifth.

♩ ♩

FIGURE 5.1

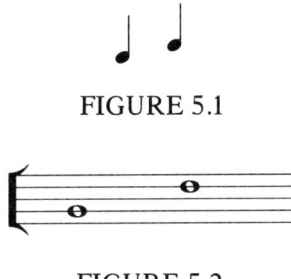

FIGURE 5.2

A competent pianist does not identify note namcs and then push down the proper two keys; rather, he or she instinctively measures within the hand the distance of, for example, a perfect fifth. The distance is to be felt, although it can be measured in literal inches. The shape of the hand is affected by the color combination of the interval. For example, let us assume that the pianist is using fingers 1 and 3 to play the interval of a major third. The hand will need to make a different adjustment to play C to E (all white notes) from that used to play D to F-sharp (a white note and a black note). This adjustment becomes more noticeable with different fingering combinations, such as substituting fingers 1 and 2 or substituting fingers 1 and 4 in the same exercise.

The following exercise will help you learn the feel of keyboard distances that form various intervals.

1. Using the interval of a perfect fifth as an example, do the following:
   a. Play a perfect fifth with fingers 1 and 5, either hand.
   b. Hold until you have a strong sense or feel of that shape.

    c. Leave your hand in that shape; lift it off the keyboard and move it right or left.

    d. Without looking down, drop your hand—still in the shape of a perfect fifth—onto the keyboard. Your hand should be playing another perfect fifth. If it is not, repeat steps a–d.

2. Play an octave and follow the preceding steps.

3. Practice the same intervals with different fingers.

4. Practice the same intervals in different keys.

5. Practice different intervals.

6. Change hands.

The next step is to imagine the hand shape for a given interval before playing it. Away from the keyboard, shape your hand for a perfect fifth. Without looking at the keyboard, drop your formed hand to the piano at any pitch or register. Still not looking at the keyboard, use your ear to determine accuracy. If the interval is incorrect, readjust your hand and try again. Do not look at the keyboard at any time throughout this exercise.

With practice, this process becomes very reliable, and your hands will seem to think for themselves as you are playing. Their independence frees the mind to cover larger landmarks of a musical score.

Exercises in Horizontal Interval Reading

For Figure 5.3, do the following exercises:

1. Identify the intervals between the notes (at X), X = 56.

2. Increase speed by increments to X = 112.

3. Without speaking the interval, scan the line to identify each interval. Aim for X = 138.

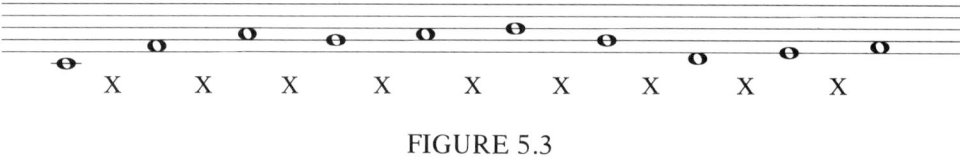

FIGURE 5.3

Figure 5.4 is the same melody as Figure 5.3. Taking each clef in order, do the following exercises:

1. Identify only the first note.

2. Read the intervals, following steps 1 and 2 for Figure 5.3.

3. Play the intervals, still identifying no note names except the first.

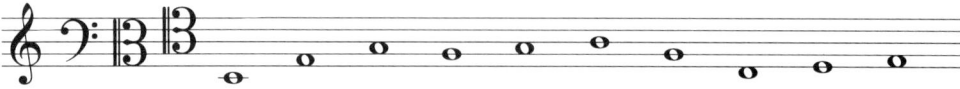

FIGURE 5.4

Figure 5.5 includes accidentals.

1. When speaking the intervals, proceed more slowly than before to allow time for the extra words. Then scan in the same tempo as before.
2. Now "play" the intervals either on a hard surface or in the air. Measure the intervals; then, check yourself on the keyboard for accuracy of feel.
3. Repeat step 2, but use different fingerings.
4. Change hands.

FIGURE 5.5

Follow the same procedure for Figure 5.6:

1. Speak the intervals.
2. Scan the intervals.
3. Pretend to play; then, check.
4. Use different fingerings.
5. Change hands.

FIGURE 5.6

Examples for Horizontal Reading

Figure 5.7 can be seen instantly as a scale. Note names past the first pitch are unimportant.

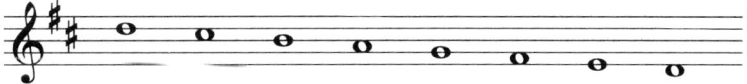

FIGURE 5.7

Figure 5.8 should also be seen instantly as a scale. The added information (meter, rhythms, and stem direction) should not befuddle you so that you perceive only small units. If you initially read only small parts such as those in Figure 5.9, then try the soft-eye exercise (page 21). Look at the G in measure 2; while your eyes remain softly on the G, let them take in the entire phrase.

FIGURE 5.8

FIGURE 5.9

Without playing Figure 5.8, practice the reading-ahead exercise described in Chapter 3:

1. At the second beat of each measure, your eyes must move to the following measure while you recall the remainder of the previous measure:

FIGURE 5.10

2. At the second beat of measure 1, move your eyes to measure 3 as you recall the remainder of measures 1 and 2.

FIGURE 5.11

Glance for a few seconds at the Beethoven theme in Figure 5.12. You will see two things:

1. It has two broken chords, f minor and C major (shown in brackets).
2. Each broken chord is followed by three short, descending diatonic patterns from A-flat, B-flat, and A-flat beneath slurs.

During this silent scanning, your hand should be feeling and sensing what your eyes are seeing.

FIGURE 5.12   Ludwig van Beethoven, fragment from *Sonata*, Op. 2, No. 1

The only other truly necessary details to note are key signature (perceiving which black notes are called for is more physical than remembering which notes are altered) and first pitch. The phrase could now be played without further study, playing every two measures from recall. Play at ○ = 40.

The articulations and the dynamics have been removed because they are not important at this point. As your reading ability improves, their importance increases.

Whether you are playing by reading or by recall, the only important things now are continuity and absolute awareness of the beat.

Glance for about two seconds at the Schumann song in Figure 5.13. You will see the following:

1. Measure 3 spans a major sixth.

2. Measure 5 spans a minor sixth.

3. Measures 4 and 5 contain three-note diatonic patterns that link the two broken chords.

4. Measure 4 gives time to scan and regroup.

FIGURE 5.13   Robert Schumann, fragment
from *Familien-Gemälde*, Op. 34, No. 4
Used by permission of C. F. Peters Corporation, New York.

Scan the example again, taking note of the preceding points. Then try to play from recall instead of playing what you are reading; for example, read measure 4 while playing measure 5. Feel the shapes in the hand before playing. Change hands.

TRANSPOSITION OF THE TENOR LINE

The tenor line in any vocal music must be transposed down one octave to be in concert pitch. Inexperienced readers usually have difficulty with this transposition; with practice, it becomes second nature. At the outset, one sees and recognizes one thing, then immediately thinks and executes another. Fluent transposition omits the first step; one will immediately think the tenor at the lower octave without stopping to recognize its written pitch. Practice Figure 5.14, as follows:

1. With your left hand, play the tenor line transposed down one octave. Use tempo ♩ = 52.

2. Play the tenor with your left hand and the soprano with your right hand. The tempo should be ♩ = 46.

3. Play both tenor and soprano with either hand alone ($\textbf{d}$ = 48).

4. Play the tenor with your right hand against the bass line of the piano accompaniment ($\textbf{d}$ = 40–48).

5. Play the accompaniment while another student plays the vocal lines, or vice versa ($\textbf{d}$ = 48–52).

6. Play the vocal lines with your right hand and the bass line from the accompaniment with your left hand ($\textbf{d}$ = 42).

FIGURE 5.14   Robert Schumann, from *Familien-Gemälde*, Op. 34, No. 4
Used by permission of C. F. Peters Corporation, New York.

FIGURE 5.14, continued

FIGURE 5.14, continued

Figure 5.15 provides further practice in transposing tenor lines down one octave. After practicing the tenor lines alone, practice Bass I and Bass II together. Then combine all four vocal parts.

Below the vocal score is a piano reduction. (Remember to transpose the right hand down an octave.) If the vocal score is troublesome to read, practice in two-measure segments, first reading the piano reduction and then the same segment from the vocal score.

FIGURE 5.15   Johannes Brahms, from *O Süsser Mai!* ("O Lovely May")

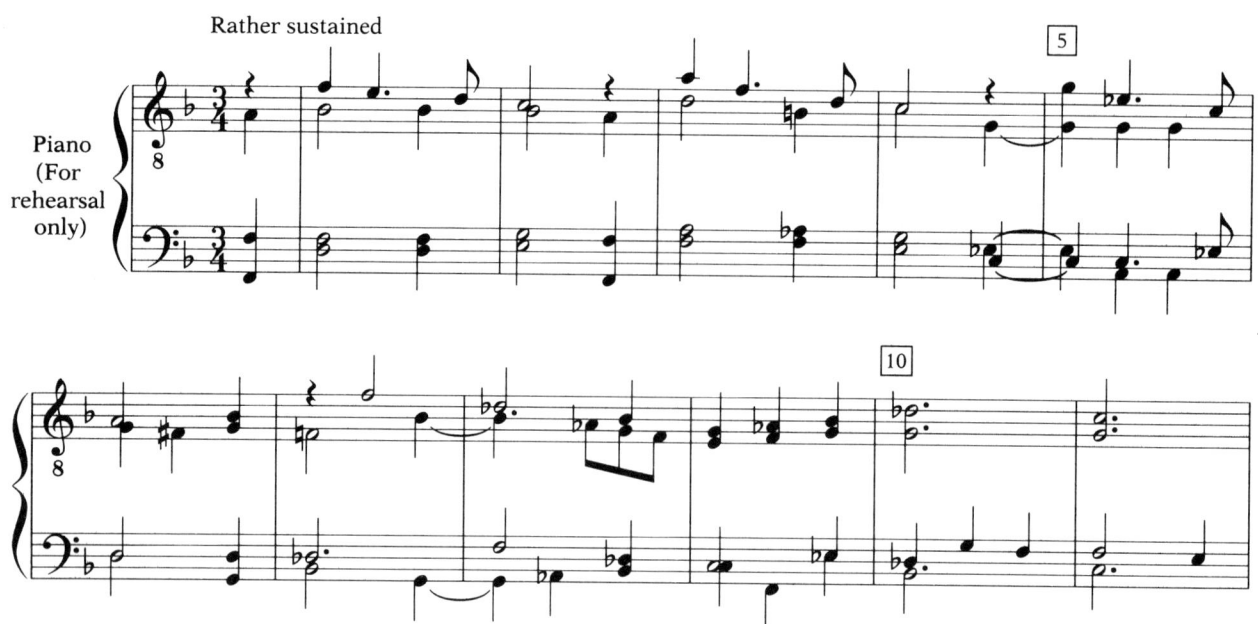

FIGURE 5.15, continued

TRANSPOSITION BY CLEFS

A significant number of this chapter's exercises involve transposition by clefs because it helps the reader to perceive horizontal lines as intervals rather than as individual notes. Many readers, especially adults, do not or cannot go beyond recognizing notes only as individual letters. The grasping of such rudimentary information as note names and their relation to the keyboard lends a false sense of security. To read with a sense of freedom, the pianist must elevate his or her perceptions to a more abstract level.

An intuitive recognition of intervallic relationships aids the reader in quickly perceiving melodic passages as broken chords or diatonic passages rather than as a string of individual notes, thus permitting the player to cover more ground both mentally and technically. Indeed, until such intuitions are active, the hand cannot prepare itself for what is to come.

Most pianists learn treble and bass clefs at a very young age, and they resist learning new clefs later on. Practice in other clefs, however, helps to develop agility of thought and immediate recognition of patterns.

Clef Substitution

Transposition may seem to have little practical value for users of this text. The reason it is dealt with here in some detail is that flexibility is stretched by seeing old things in a new way.

As an introduction to transposition in general, transposition by octave, as in the tenor line, was relatively uncomplicated; yet, it required that you read one clef while playing in another.

The following exercises go one step further by introducing transposition by clef substitution. Application of bass clef to the treble-clef line automatically transposes a treble-clef line up a third, in Figure 5.16 a major third. Notice that the melody begins on the sixth degree.

1. Scan. Notice the repeated range of an octave. Sense fingerings.

2. Recite intervals at X, X = 52.

3. Substitute bass clef for treble clef and adjust the key signature (easier after reading intervals).

4. Review the intervals. Without playing, recite the new note names, ♩ = 72, and allow your hand to silently feel the shapes of the intervals.

5. Play in the new key (♩ = 72).

6. Transpose up a minor third and follow steps 1–5.

FIGURE 5.16 Mussorgsky/Burmeister, *Pictures at an Exhibition*, Promenade

For Figure 5.17, proceed as you did for Figure 5.16, but make the first transposition up a minor third, to F major. Add the left hand in the transposed key—study the intervals and use your ear.

FIGURE 5.17   Jeremiah Clarke, *King William's March*

Figure 5.18, a fugue with a subject that is visually attractive, transposes handily up a major third, to g minor. Its intervals and diatonic passages come quickly to sight:

Measures 1–3: Perfect fifth and minor sixth fit the hand.

Measures 4–9: This passage is diatonic.

Measures 10–17: Intervals of sixths, fourths, and thirds alternate with diatonic measures.

Prepare and practice as in the preceding exercises. Then try the following:

1. Read two voices transposed to measure 32, ♩ = 60. As an accuracy check, one occasionally needs to perceive the interval between the two voices.

2. Read the entire page, transposed, as a trio, with one player to a part, ♩ = 92.

FIGURE 5.18   Dmitri Shostakovich, *Fuge XIV*
© Edition Peters, Leipzig. Used by permission of
C. F. Peters Corporation, sole selling agents.

Figure 5.19, an exercise in clef substitution, can also be a preliminary score-reading exercise. Practice as follows:

1. Transpose the horn, using bass clef and playing one octave higher for concert pitch, ♩ = 60.
2. Play the transposed horn against the piano bass line, ♩ = 60. Piano left hand can be reduced to a single-note bass line for added ease.
3. Play in a two-piano arrangement.
   a. One student plays the piano part while one student plays the horn and violin parts, ♩ = 69. (In measures 9–20, the violin may play one octave higher than written.)
   b. Use any other division suited to the students' skill.

FIGURE 5.19   Johannes Brahms, from *Trio for Piano, Violin, and Natural Horn*, Op. 40

C Clefs

Reading C clefs has several beneficial applications, but its main function here is to reinforce horizontal reading. Reading is more abstract than factual; written music is not always what it seems. The idea that a note is identified by its line or space is applicable only within the confines of a particular clef. Note names determine location on the keyboard; beyond that, shapes, intervals, and chords are more useful for quick perception of horizontal lines.

C clefs are used today for several performing instruments, especially viola, trombone, and cello, which use alto and tenor clefs. For the pianist, they are a versatile tool. Besides being useful for learning the abstractions of horizontal reading, concentration, and mental agility, they are also necessary for score reading. These C-clef exercises are a means to an end, to be studied here not for themselves but for what they can contribute to courageous reading.

The only C clefs included are alto and tenor. The other three, while useful, are more remote and less frequently used.

If you have not previously dealt with C clefs, all you need to know is that the alto-clef middle C rests on the third line and the tenor-clef middle C rests on the fourth line. (See Figure 5.20.)

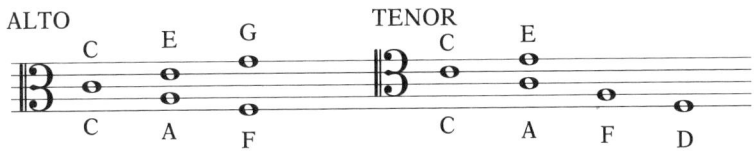

FIGURE 5.20

While reading C clefs, continue the practice of reading horizontal intervals. Learning the actual note names then becomes a tool rather than an absolute and only resource.

In the next three examples, do the following:

1. Read the intervals of the C-clef line.

2. Play the C-clef line alone; then, play together with the other lines. In three-part examples, play at least one line in each hand, the C clef always being one of them.

3. Also perceive vertical intervals between the various clefs. In three-part examples, read the full chord. Suggested places to check are marked by an X.

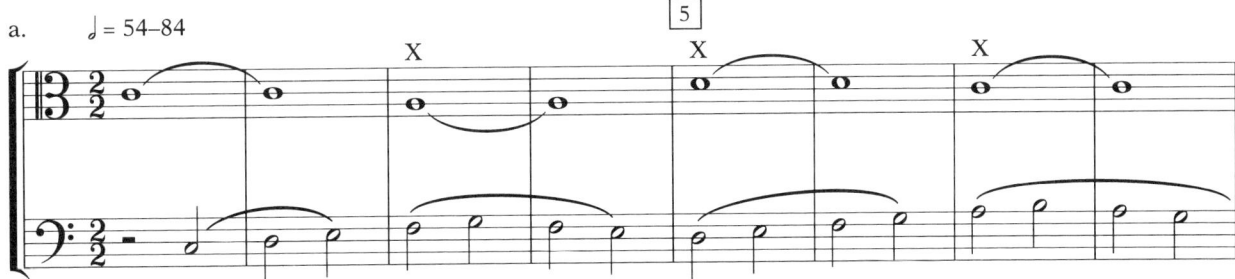

FIGURE 5.21   C. S. Lang, *Score Reading Exercises*
Copyright © 1950 Novello & Company Ltd. Used by permission of the publisher. Sole representative U.S.A., Theodore Presser Company.

FIGURE 5.21, continued

(continued)

FIGURE 5.21, continued

FIGURE 5.22   Marcello, from *Sonata in A Minor*
Reprinted from Robert A. Melcher and Willard F. Warch,
Music for Score-Reading. Copyright © 1971 by Prentice-Hall.

FIGURE 5.23   Francoeur, from *Sonata in E Major*
Reprinted from Robert A. Melcher and Willard F. Warch,
Music for Score-Reading. Copyright © 1971 by Prentice-Hall.

Three examples that were used earlier may now be used for further practice in transposition by clef. See Figures 5.16, 5.17, and 5.18. Substitution of the alto clef automatically transposes a treble-clef line up a second, the choice of major or minor being up to the player. Substitution of the tenor clef automatically transposes a treble-clef line down a major or a minor second. Follow the same preparation as before.

No clefs or key signatures are given for Figures 5.24 through 5.28. The assignment is to play each tune in four different keys by applying alto clef, tenor clef, bass clef, and treble clef in turn while chording in the left hand. Information for each tune includes the scale degree of the first pitch, indication of a major (M) or minor (m) quality, and suggested metronome markings.

Work through each melody one clef and key at a time, chording in the left hand. As the idea becomes more natural, repeat the tune without pause; the second time, play in a different clef. By playing the clefs in the order of bass, alto, treble, and tenor, you will transpose the melody downward by step; the reverse would transpose the tune upward by step.

Figure Number	Quality	Scale Degree of the First Pitch
5.27	M	5
5.28	M	3
5.29	M	1 (tonic)
5.30	M	1 (tonic)
5.31	M	1 (tonic)
5.32	M	3
5.33	M	5
5.34	M	3

FIGURE 5.24

FIGURE 5.25

FIGURE 5.26

FIGURE 5.27

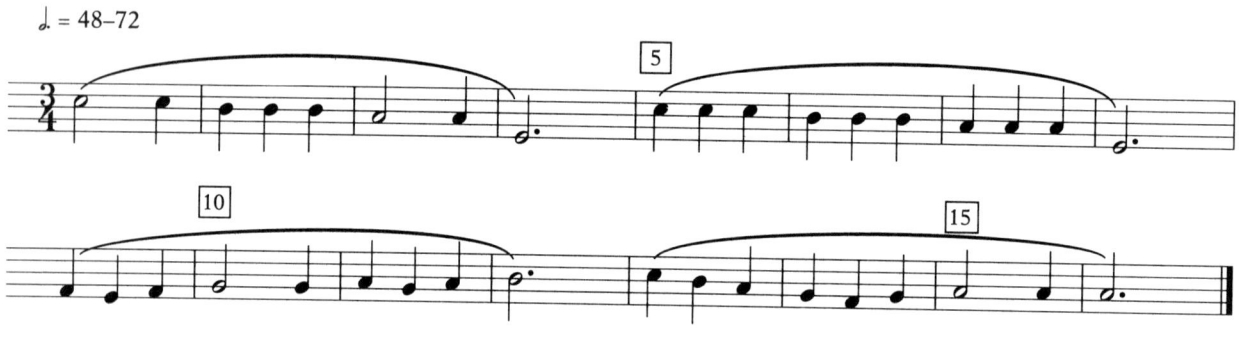

FIGURE 5.28

Figure 5.29 gives practice in reading the tenor clef and also offers the opportunity for practice in preliminary score reading. Practice in the following ways:

1. Before playing the cello line, study the horizontal intervals in detail. Recite them aloud. If not secure, recite them again while playing silently. Then play ♩ = 44.

2. Add the piano bass line. Octaves may be reduced to a single line (♩ = 44).

3. Practice the piano part.
   a. Practice the bass line without looking at the keyboard.
   b. Chord the right hand in two-beat groups.
   c. Combine a and b.
   d. Play as written.

FIGURE 5.29 Johannes Brahms, from *Quartet No. 3 in C Minor*, Op. 60

FIGURE 5.29, continued

FIGURED BASS

As are C clefs, these figured bass exercises are a means to an end. They combine horizontal intervals with vertical intervals in a particular way, which for some students sparks an awareness of horizontal reading that other exercises do not.

The following practice suggestions should clarify why figured bass is included here as part of horizontal reading instead of in Chapter 6, "Vertical Reading."

Throughout the examples, the student is asked to sing the figured part and also to play it as a single melodic line. These two applications force the reader to also think, hear, and feel horizontally.

The bass line in Figure 5.30 is a pedal-point C, which introduces the vertical relationships in an easier fashion than does a moving bass line. However, when one isolates the figured line as a single voice, as in Figure 5.31, its intervals become purely horizontal.

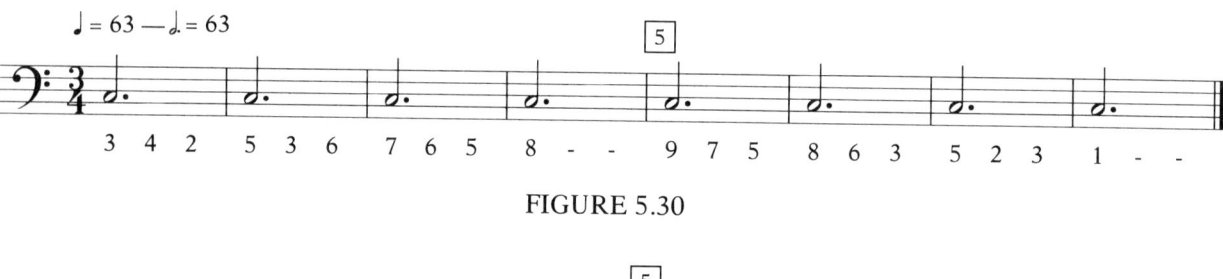

FIGURE 5.30

FIGURE 5.31

Additionally, applying the following four practice suggestions to Figures 5.30 and 5.31 should clarify horizontal perceptions in figured bass.

1. Sing the figured line, first determining the starting pitch.

2. Play the figured line.

3. Notate the figured line.

4. Define the horizontal intervals. Measures 1–5 of Figure 5.31 are given here.

|¹3 (↑m2) 4 (↓m3) 2 (↑P4) |²5 (↓m3) 3 (↑P4) 6 (↑M2)
|³7 (↓M2) 6 (↓M2) 5 (↑P4) |⁴8 (↑M2) | ⁵9 (↓M3) 7 (↓M3) 5 (↑P4)|

These four applications can be followed in any order.

As you practice the five two-voice exercises in Figure 5.32, draw as necessary from the previous four suggestions. In addition, experiment with the following ideas:

1. Play the bass line and sing the figured line.

2. Play as a duet, one student on bass and one on figured line.

3. Play both voices in one hand.

4. Increase the tempo.

FIGURE 5.32   Helen Keaney, from *Figured Bass for Beginners*, two parts
Copyright © 1981 by E. C. Schirmer, Boston.

As you practice the five three-voice exercises of Figure 5.33, again draw from all the preceding suggestions, but also try the following:

1. Play as a trio, one student on bass and one each on the two figured lines.

2. Sing one of the figured parts while playing the other figured part and the bass line.

a.   ♩ = 54 — 𝅗𝅥 = 44

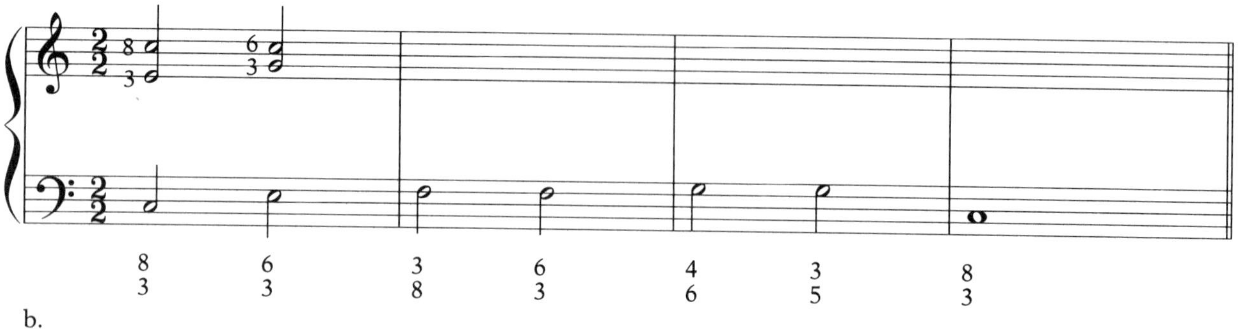

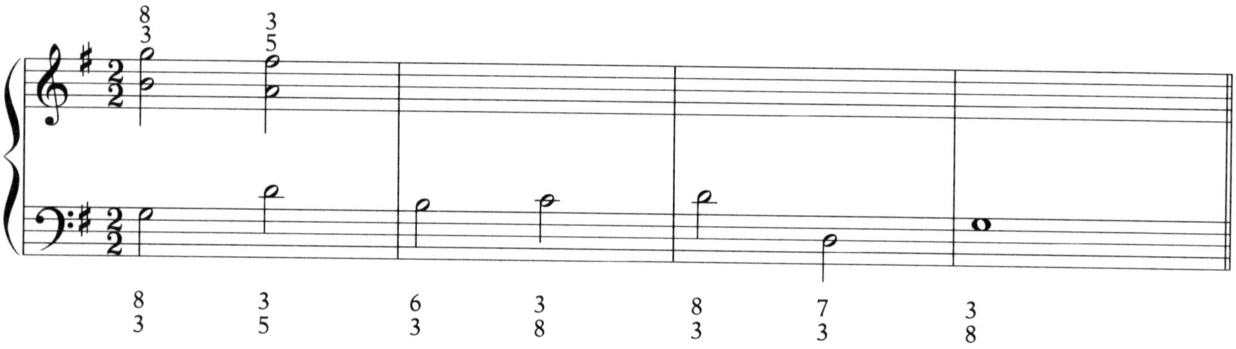

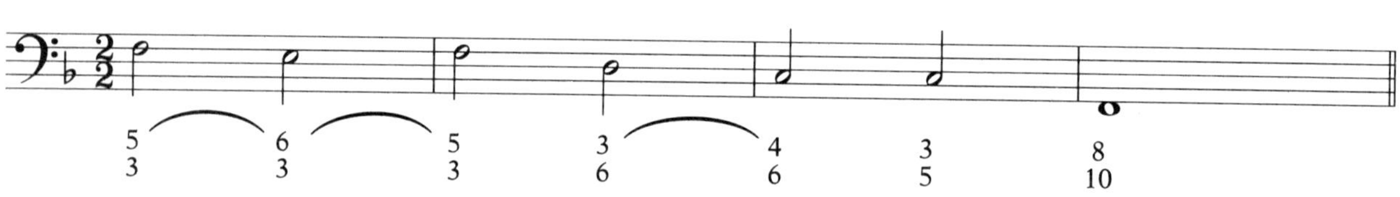

FIGURE 5.33   Helen Keaney, from *Figured Bass for Beginners*, two parts
Copyright © 1981 by E. C. Schirmer, Boston.

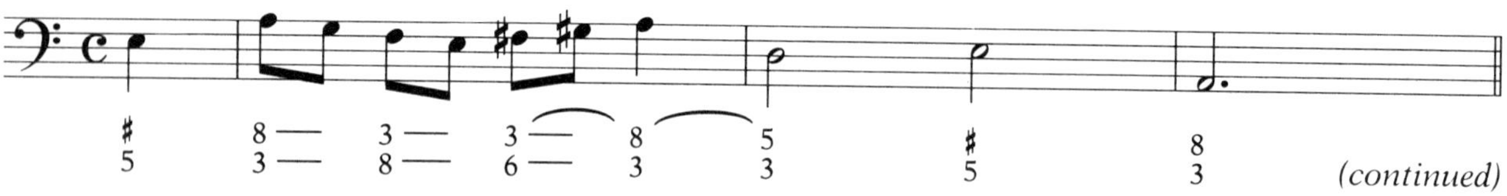

(continued)

e.

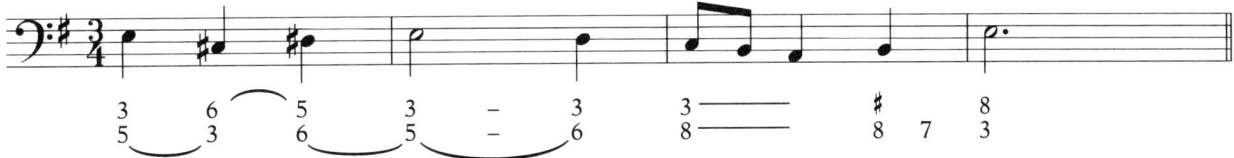

FIGURE 5.33, continued

Keyboard Feel

We have already emphasized that a pianist must feel what he or she sees, even before playing it. Throughout the text, the necessity for keyboard feel is implied, if not directly stated. In mastering the subjects of Chapters 4 and 5—contact and horizontal intervals—you should move from mental and aural awareness to tactile perceptions. You can do much practice without using a keyboard. The muscles are practicing even as we only think of a phrase. In ear-training tests, many pianists confirm the interval they hear by feeling it in their hands. The feel is invisible; an observer will see no hand movement as the mind and the body work together.[1]

A brief exercise is presented to help reinforce the point. Study the two measures of Figure 5.34. Make physical note of each hand's rhythm, possibly tapping each hand alone and then hands together. Make careful observations about the fingering, especially in the right hand, and define the fingering you expect to use. *Feel* the intervals and relate them to your fingerings. Several fingerings are possible for the right hand—you just need to feel which one you intend to use. Be especially sensitive to the location of black notes. After a minute or two of silent study, play the example once. If what you planned did not work, then apply these ideas to a different snippet of music. Do not practice these two measures until you get it "right." One chance is all that is allowed.

FIGURE 5.34

NOTE

1. Charles A. Garfield and Hal Zina Bennett, *Peak Performance: Mental Training Techniques of the World's Greatest Athletes* (Los Angeles: Warner Books, 1984), pp. 16–17.

CHAPTER SIX

Vertical Reading

HARMONIC READING

Many players are discouraged at the first sight of any score. Open score looks monstrous; piano score often strikes fear in a reader's heart before the hands ever reach the keyboard. Even relatively simple music contains hundreds of bits of information that baffle and defeat the inexperienced or fearful reader. Such readers see all of this information literally and try their best to be accurate and complete in every detail of the notes. Rhythm then inevitably suffers and is, for some reason, the "detail" overlooked.

Education in general and music training in particular tend to teach strict adherence to factual detail, usually punishing oversights and mistakes. In this chapter, only two errors are possible: seeing details instead of large harmonic patterns and inconsistent rhythm. The goal is to teach you to perceive very large harmonic patterns and reduce detail to a minimum. In fact, you may actually overlook some details. For example, fluent readers are often unaware of note letters as they play. Their reactions are to shapes, distances, feel, and direction. You will scan scores and see them harmonically, so that you will perceive a chord as a single entity rather than as made up of several parts. Figures 6.1 and 6.2 clarify this act of harmonic reading.

In Figure 6.1, notice that parts c, d, and f do not account for the inversions. The chords are called in root position. Inversions are another aspect of clutter.

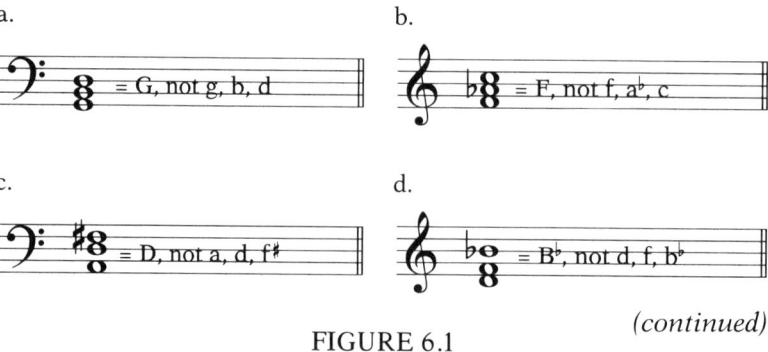

FIGURE 6.1   *(continued)*

111

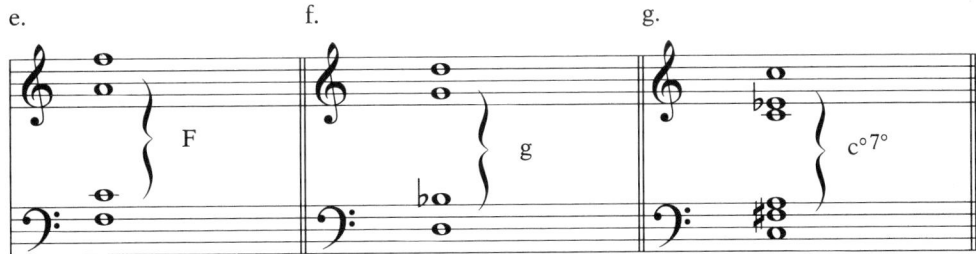

FIGURE 6.1, continued

To apply harmonic scanning to a musical example, examine the following four-part score and its analysis (Figure 6.2).

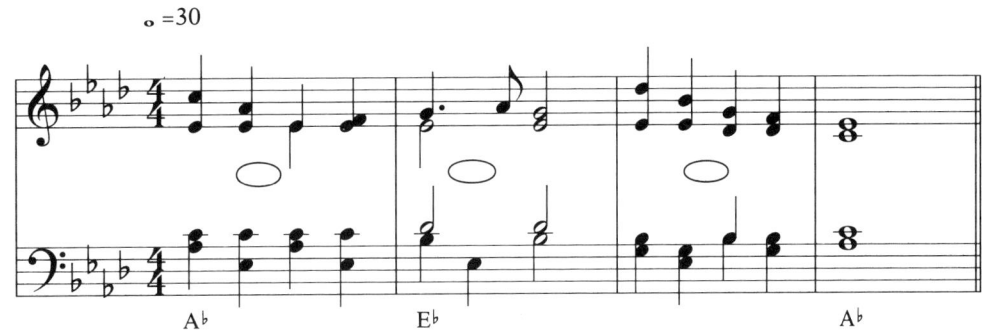

FIGURE 6.2

Many details are omitted in the large analysis—for example:

Measure 1: root positions and inversions, added sixth on beat 4

Measure 2: second inversions and nonharmonic tone

Measure 3: inversions, incomplete harmony on beat 3, unclear harmony on beat 4

In performance, most of these details would be played. At this point, however, it doesn't matter if they are not. The basic outlines of the music are still present. When playing, let your eyes rest on the large oval in the middle of each measure and move lightly from one oval to the next.

In the chorale-style exercises of Figures 6.3 through 6.7, practice silent harmonic reading, using these basic guidelines:

1. Read the harmonic rhythm aloud.

2. Let your eyes move easily from measure to measure.

3. Read from the bottom up.

4. Rhythm is extremely important (practice with a metronome and adjust the tempo as necessary). If you cannot identify a chord in the time allowed, skip it and move on to the next chord without losing any beats. *Rhythm is more important than notes.* Practice with a metronome to help establish consistent and uninterrupted rhythm.

Play the exercises, applying the preceding guidelines. The following variations help to build self-reliance.

1. Have one student recite the harmony in rhythm while a second student plays the harmony (the player will not have a score). The voicing is unimportant—try to have at least two voices in each hand. Adjust the tempo as necessary.

2. Repeat step 1, but have the player play with eyes closed.

3. If the first playing was mostly in root position, repeat and try to make the bass line more sophisticated.

4. Read the score, reciting each harmony before playing it. Use a slower tempo if necessary.

5. Play normally, but retain a strong internal understanding of harmony as you play.

6. Play with a conductor.

The diagrams in Figures 6.3 and 6.5 help to explain what is meant by harmonic rhythm.

In measures 1–6 of Figure 6.4, a relatively slow harmonic rhythm moves against an active melodic rhythm.

Let your eyes move rhythmically from harmony to harmony. Read from the bottom up.

Melodic rhythm

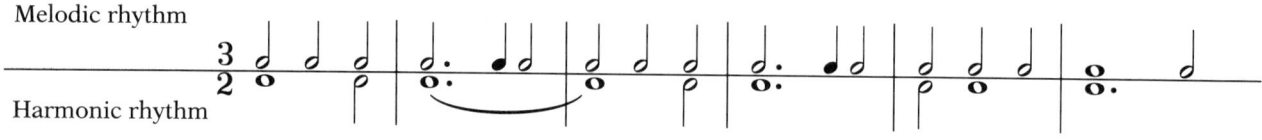

Harmonic rhythm

FIGURE 6.3

(continued)

FIGURE 6.4 Giuseppe Ottavio Pitoni, *Laudate Dominum*

FIGURE 6.4, continued

Melodic rhythm

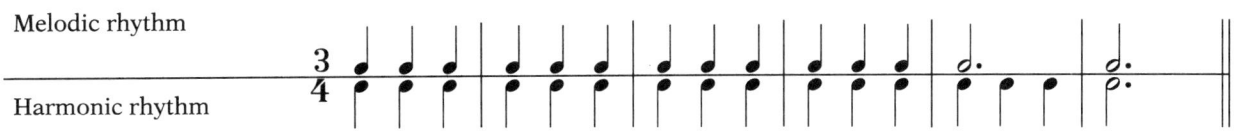

Harmonic rhythm

FIGURE 6.5

The harmonic rhythm in Figure 6.6 is synchronized exactly with the overall rhythm of the music.

While you are speaking or playing a chord, your eyes should be on the next chord.

While practicing these exercises, remember the basic rules: (1) Take no notice of inversions; (2) speak only the letter name of each chord—the quality need not be spoken; (3) eyes must move rhythmically from harmony to harmony; and (4) *rhythm must be continuous*.

FIGURE 6.6   Peter Sohren, *Chorale*

FIGURE 6.6, continued

To reinforce the feeling of harmonic reading in Figure 6.7, tie those notes that are common between chords.

FIGURE 6.7   Menegali, *Jesu Salvator Mundi*
Reprinted from Robert A. Melcher and Willard F. Warch,
Music for Score-Reading. Copyright © 1971 by Prentice-Hall.

Polyphonic music is the best combination of simultaneous vertical and horizontal reading. Contrapuntal music, such as Figure 6.8, makes regular harmonic reading impractical; yet, if vertical harmonies are not taken into consideration, note-by-note reading returns. Practice Figure 6.8, reciting harmonies at the X's before and during playing. Also do the following:

1. Write in fingerings. The middle voice may be distributed between the two hands.

2. Sing the part best suited to your voice as you play the other two parts.

FIGURE 6.8   Byrd, *Non Nobis, Domine*
Reprinted from Robert A. Melcher and Willard F. Warch,
Music for Score-Reading. Copyright © 1971 by Prentice-Hall.

Figure 6.9 is the same piece as Figure 6.4, page 113, where it was condensed. Students should remember that in choral scores, the tenor line must be transposed down one octave. If necessary, review Chapter 5, pages 90–91, and Figures 5.14 and 5.15. Figure 6.10 provides further practice in transposition.

(continued)

FIGURE 6.9   Giuseppe Ottavio Pitoni, *Laudate Dominum*, for mixed chorus, a cappella

FIGURE 6.9, continued

♩ = 56–63

FIGURE 6.10   Arcadelt, *Ave Maria*
Reprinted from Robert A. Melcher and Willard F. Warch,
Music for Score-Reading. Copyright © 1971 by Prentice-Hall.

FIGURE 6.10, continued

(continued)

FIGURE 6.10, continued

Figure 6.11 continues practice in harmonic reading, but because of its many accidentals, you must take more precise care to ensure accuracy.

FIGURE 6.11   Vincent Persichetti, *Hymns and Responses*, No. 1
© 1956 Elkan-Vogel, Inc. Used by permission of the
publisher. Sole representative—Theodore Presser Company.

Figure 6.12 goes one step further than the preceding examples for harmonic reading. Because of its relatively complex Romantic harmony and the many accidentals, suspensions, and passing tones, a literal harmonic recitation is not practical. In this case, read with a general sense of the underlying harmony but without necessarily accounting for every tone. A few measures of suggested harmonic reading are presented to give you the idea—notice that many of the non-harmonic tones are not accounted for. The specificity of the harmonic reading encountered in the earlier exercises should become a fundamental technique without being literal and restricting. Also practice Figures 6.13 and 6.14.

FIGURE 6.12 Richard Wagner, *Trauersinfonie* on Themes by C. M. von Weber
Reprinted from Joseph A. Labuta, *Basic Conducting
Techniques*. Copyright © 1982 by Prentice-Hall.

FIGURE 6.12, continued

♩ = 56–72

Allegro maestoso e vivace

FIGURE 6.13   Franz Schubert, *Mass in A-flat*, Credo

FIGURE 6.13, continued

(continued)

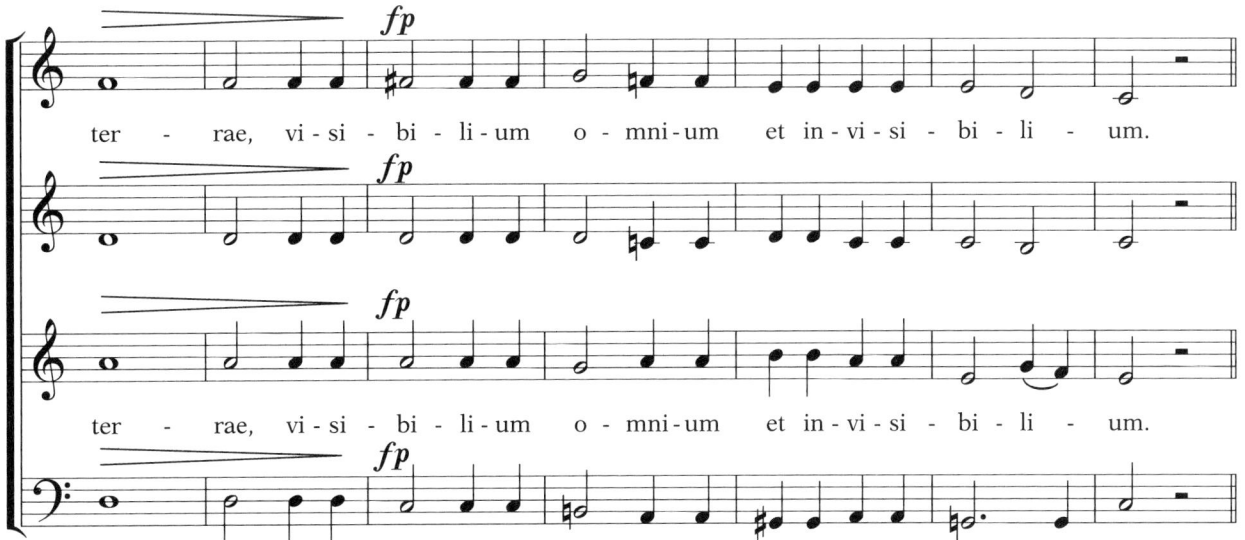

FIGURE 6.13, continued

FIGURE 6.14   W. A. Mozart, from *Ave Verum*

FIGURE 6.14, continued

For Figure 6.15, do the following:

1. Practice any two parts interchangeably. Then practice three, then four, parts.

2. Apply recited harmony procedures.

3. Tie all repeated tones.

4. Conversely, play all repeated tones with a brisk staccato. Moving voices will be legato.

FIGURE 6.15   Johannes Brahms, *Liebeslieder Walzer*, Op. 52, No. 8
Reprinted from Robert A. Melcher and Willard F. Warch,
Music for Score-Reading. Copyright © 1971 by Prentice-Hall.

In Vivaldi's *Magnificat* (Figure 6.16), the corresponding piano reduction is directly across from the choral segment. Practice as you did Figure 6.15. You may utilize various other practice techniques, such as these:

1. Read the choral score, any two parts, one part per hand (♩ = 72).

2. Read the four-part choral score. Alternate with the piano reduction as necessary to facilitate learning (♩ = 52).

3. Sing one of the parts as you play (♩ = 52).

4. Play the reduction or the score for a conductor (♩ = 63).

Be sure to include harmonic recitation in rhythm as part of the preparation.

FIGURE 6.16 Antonio Vivaldi, *Magnificat*, Chorus

(continued)

FIGURE 6.16, continued

FIGURE 6.16, continued

Figure 6.17 is a second copy of the *Magnificat* and includes the orchestra score between the choral score and its piano reduction. Practice in the following ways:

1. One person on choral score
2. One or two persons on orchestra score
3. One person on piano reduction
4. One person conducting

Perform, switch parts, and play again.

FIGURE 6.17   Antonio Vivaldi, *Magnificat*

FIGURE 6.17, continued

(continued)

FIGURE 6.17, continued

Different Perceptions of One Piece

Sight reading is a composite of many skills. This text has examined many of them one-by-one, isolating each problem and designing techniques for mastering each skill. The next four examples represent the same piece (Figure 6.22) in four different ways. Most of the techniques have been covered earlier; Figure 6.20, fake book, is the exception. Before looking at the original piece, work through the examples, following instructions for each one as needed.

Figure 6.18: Harmonic Recitation

1. Play the exercise, two voices in each hand (♩ = 56). The base line is unimportant. The rhythmic notation is applied to the harmonic rhythm.

2. While one person recites letter names in rhythm, a second person plays the chords (♪= 60). The player uses neither score nor exercise; this is a keyboard dictation exercise.

3. Repeat step 2, but have the pianist play with eyes closed.

4. Tie repeated tones.

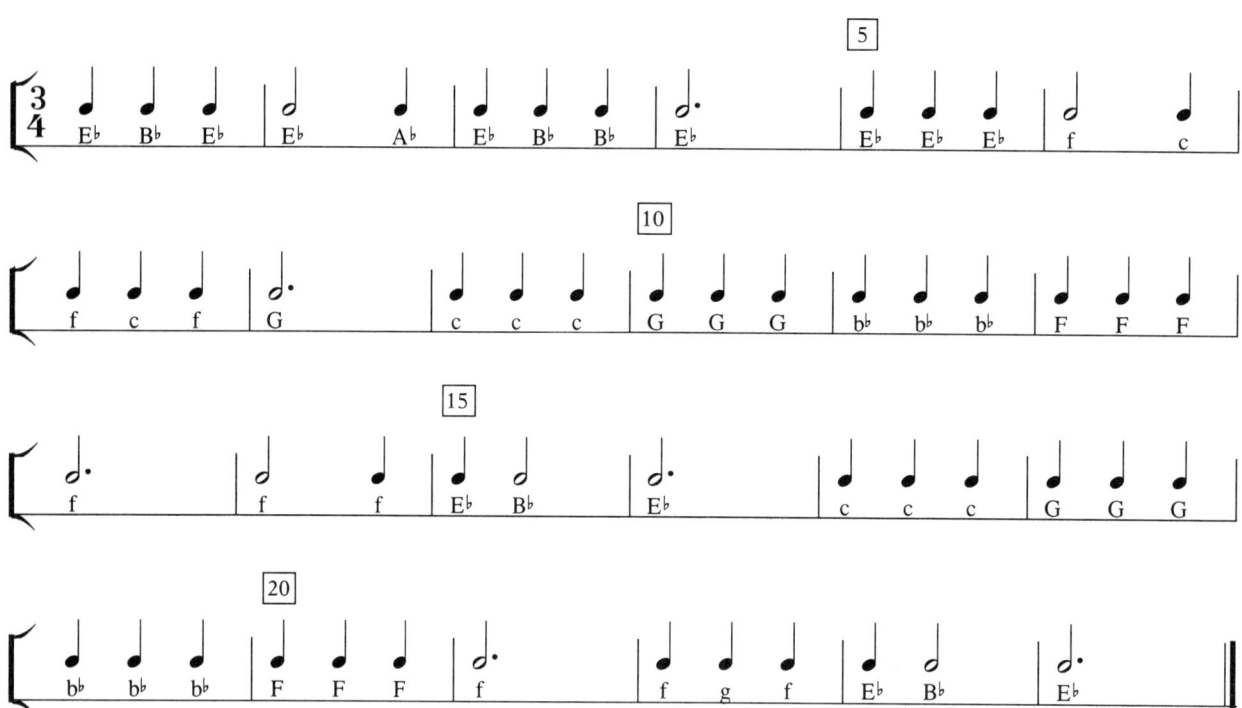

FIGURE 6.18   Harmonic Recitation

Figure 6.19: Figured Bass

1. Recite root-position letter names to the figured bass line (♩ = 48).
2. Play the bass line; recite as before (♩ = 54).
3. Realize the bass line, two voices in each hand (♩ = 48).

FIGURE 6.19   Figured Bass

Figure 6.20: Fake Book

1. Play the melody and the bass line (♩ = 69).
2. With the left hand alone, fill in the chords in the bass line (♩ = 63).
3. Play (♩ = 69). Be sure the bass line is accurate. Follow the symbols literally.

Fake book symbols are understood as:

chord/bass note; for example, E♭/G = E♭ chord in 1st inversion: E♭$_6$

FIGURE 6.20   Fake Book

Figure 6.21: Score Expansion with Alto Clef

1. Read the letter names of each chord (♩ = 50).
2. Play the score (no rhythm defined), saying the chord before playing it.
3. Play at a comfortable tempo (♩ = 66).
4. Play for a conductor.

FIGURE 6.21   Score Expansion with Alto Clef

(continued)

FIGURE 6.21, continued

Figure 6.22 is the original piano piece from which the preceding exercises were extracted. Practice it in its original form in the following ways:

1. Finger for maximum contact and efficiency.
2. Release notes where needed for re-articulation.
3. Recite harmonies while playing.
4. Make it beautiful.

FIGURE 6.22   Genari Karganov, *Prayer*, Op. 25, No. 5

CHAPTER SEVEN

Score Reading

Root-position chords in one hand are the bare bones of harmonic reading. Open score is the opposite extreme, and piano score occupies middle ground. Open-score reading, when done by a fine reader, is a mysterious process to observe. It involves great talent, intuition, and technique.

Open-score reading would seem to require more advanced skill than could be expected of students who are at the reading level of this book; nevertheless, its basic elements—agile eyes, contact, continuity, harmonic reading, C clefs, and transpositions—have already been introduced. It is now time to gain an understanding of the entry level of the skill. To approach score reading, we present several short exercises, which cover the following subjects:

1. Reduction of clutter
2. Redistribution of parts
3. Omissions
4. Expansion-contraction
5. Orchestra and band scores, with procedural instructions

REDUCTION OF CLUTTER

Earlier exercises taught finger independence and contact through practice in tying tones common between chords. Figure 7.1 continues that practice, but for a different reason—to assist the reader in reducing the clutter of notes by minimizing the reading effort. This technique assumes ability in harmonic recitation.

Play the exercise first, tying the notes as indicated. Then play it a second time, as written, without ties, but let your eyes read in one-measure groups rather than in one-beat harmonies.

FIGURE 7.1   G. F. Handel, *Xerxes,* "Largo"
Reprinted from Joseph A. Labuta, *Basic Conducting
Techniques.* Copyright © 1982 by Prentice-Hall.

In Figure 7.2, recite harmonies on downbeats at a tempo of ♩. = 30. If you are unable to determine the harmony in time, omit that downbeat and move ahead in rhythm. Increase speed to ♩. = 40.

Perform with one player to a part, each player calling out downbeat harmonies, ♪ = 84–112.

FIGURE 7.2   J. S. Bach, *The Well-Tempered Clavier*, Fuga XI
Reprinted by permission of Belwin-Mills Publishing
Company c/o CPP/Belwin, Inc. Miami, FL 33014.

FIGURE 7.2, continued

(continued)

FIGURE 7.2, continued

FIGURE 7.2, continued

REDISTRIBUTION OF PARTS

Piano players, even in solo literature, often redistribute the parts between the hands in a way different from what is written. Usually, they do so to more easily execute a difficult passage or to avoid unsatisfactory omissions. The four brief passages that follow are examples of possible redistribution. The notes above the heavy black line should be taken by the right hand, and those below the heavy black line should be taken by the left hand.

FIGURE 7.3   Carl Maria von Weber, *Sonata No. 2*, Andante

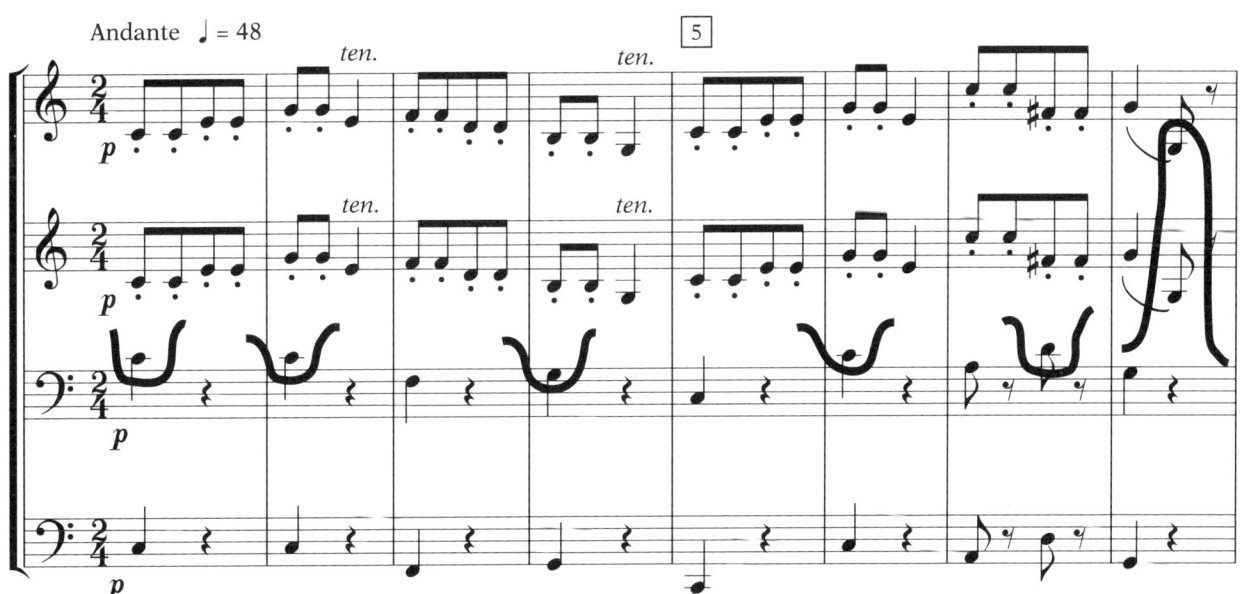

FIGURE 7.4   Franz Joseph Haydn, *Symphony No. 94*, second movement
Reprinted from Joseph A. Labuta, *Basic Conducting Techniques*. Copyright © 1982 by Prentice-Hall.

FIGURE 7.5   Richard Rodgers, from *Victory at Sea*
Copyright © by Hal Leonard Publishing.

REDISTRIBUTION OF PARTS

FIGURE 7.6 Antonin Dvořák, *Symphony No. 9*, Finale
Reprinted from Joseph A. Labuta, *Basic Conducting Techniques*. Copyright © 1982 by Prentice-Hall.

OMISSIONS

When reading a score, whether open score, partially condensed score, or piano reduction, it is necessary to omit certain parts. They may be technically unplayable, or they may require unreachable intervals, or they may simply be uncomfortable. Sometimes it is better to play nothing than to play an obvious error. Such decisions are instantaneous. Figures 7.7 and 7.8 are presented to give students actual practice in omitting written material because it is impossible to play everything on the page.

Our education system teaches total accuracy at all times under risk of penalty. Here, however, penalties are incurred only for interruptions of rhythm. Omit whatever and whenever necessary to maintain the motion, tailoring what you see to your technical level.

After rehearsing these exercises privately, play them with a conductor.

(continued)

FIGURE 7.7   John Cacavas, *Rhapsodic Essay*
Copyright © MCMLXIV by Carl Fischer, Inc.

FIGURE 7.7, continued

FIGURE 7.8 Hilmar F. Luckhardt, *Analogue Overture*
Used with permission of Neil A. Kjos Music Company, 1989.

FIGURE 7.8, continued

FIGURE 7.8, continued

EXPANSION-CONTRACTION

Both piano music and orchestra music are harmonically and melodically complete within themselves. Orchestra score reduces into piano score and, likewise, piano score expands into orchestra score. Two notable examples are Mussorgsky's *Pictures at an Exhibition* for piano, transcribed for orchestra by Ravel, and Ravel's *Le Tombeau de Couperin* for piano, transcribed by the composer for orchestra (except the last movement, a toccata, which is purely piano music). Beethoven's piano sonatas through Opus 31 could be handily arranged for string quartet; indeed, Opus 14, No. 1, *is* set for both piano and quartet. Mozart's sonata writing often sounds as if it is drawn from an opera overture. Schubert's sonatas sound orchestral.

Figures 7.9 through 7.12 illustrate expansion and contraction of score. Here, piano pieces have been stretched into four parts. As with previous choral scores, alternate between reading piano score and reading the arranged score if necessary. Do not, however, become too reliant on the piano score; rather, take the arranged version as slowly as necessary, but maintain continuity.

FIGURE 7.9   Robert Schumann, *Album for the Young*, "Schnitterliedchen," Op. 68, No. 18

FIGURE 7.10   Robert Schumann, *"Schnitterliedchen,"* scored version

(continued)

FIGURE 7.10, continued

FIGURE 7.11   Robert Schumann, *Album for the Young,* "Thema," Op. 68, No. 34

Langsam mit inniger empfindung   ♪ = 52–66

FIGURE 7.12   Robert Schumann, "Thema," scored version, arr. E. Burmeister

FIGURE 7.12, continued

(continued)

FIGURE 7.12, continued

FIGURE 7.12, continued

SCORE

As preparation for playing *Old Hundredth* (Figure 7.13), do the following:

1. Practice flute, low brass, and woodwind lines, at ♩ = 60.

2. Transpose the alto saxophone line, using bass clef. Then play the transposed alto sax line with flute and low brass lines (♩ = 60).

3. Transpose the clarinet and cornet lines, using tenor clef. Play the transposed lines with flute and low brass lines (♩ = 52).

4. The French horn line may be transposed using mezzo-soprano clef. Since mezzo-soprano clef is not included in this textbook, either omit the French horn line or use intervallic transposition.

5. Practice harmonic recitation reading from the bottom up, ♩ = 46.

FIGURE 7.13 Louis Bourgeois, *Old Hundredth*

FIGURE 7.13, continued

The Haydn score of Figure 7.14 and the band score of Figure 7.13 include specific suggestions for pre-practice. Instead of similarly pre-practicing Figure 7.14 by playing various parts, prepare only by scanning. The scanning will take longer than for previous exercises; instead of seconds, it may take a couple of minutes, but it should stop short of study. Notice the following things:

1. Doublings: High woodwinds often double high strings. Low woodwinds often double low strings.

2. Redistributions: In measure 5, the 2nd violin line is now taken in the left hand.

3. Modifications: In measure 5, the 2nd violin line can play quarters. In measure 17, the viola line can play quarters.

4. Omissions: In measure 36, the string parts may be omitted because the woodwind parts are easier, or the woodwind parts may be omitted because the string parts are more interesting. From measure 36 on, omit the appoggiaturas unless you know how to execute them.

5. Large designs: In measures 44–47, there are scales in the low string parts.

FIGURE 7.14   Franz Joseph Haydn, from *Sinfonia No. 91*

FIGURE 7.14, continued

FIGURE 7.14, continued

ANNOTATED BIBLIOGRAPHY

BERKOWITZ, SOL. *Improvisation Through Keyboard Harmony*. Englewood Cliffs, N.J.: Prentice-Hall, 1975. 220 pages.
> A fifteen-chapter book covering basic triads, secondary sevenths, diminished sevenths, modulations, figured bass, jazz chord notation, and so on.

FERGUSON, HOWARD, and R. O. MORRIS. *Preparatory Exercises in Score-Reading*. London: Oxford University Press, 1931. 110 pages.
> C clefs in two, three, and four parts as well as orchestral excerpts.

HAYDN, FRANZ JOSEPH. *Twelve Symphonies* arranged for piano, four hands, by Hugo Ulrich; Book I, Book II. New York: G. Schirmer, 1983.
> Excellent arrangements playable by intermediate pianists.

KEANEY, HELEN. *Figured Bass for Beginners*. Boston: E. C. Schirmer, 1981. 68 pages.
> Begins with easiest possible exercises for figured bass. Expands gradually from two parts to full-textured examples from repertoire. Stresses intervallic thinking.

KERN, ALICE M. *Harmonization and Transposition at the Keyboard*. Evanston, Ill.: Summy-Birchard, 1963; revised 1968. 128 pages. Currently out of print.
> Melodies are organized according to the harmony they require: I V7; I IV V7; minors; secondary triads; secondary dominants; and so on.

LABUTA, JOSEPH A. *Basic Conducting Techniques*. 2nd ed. Englewood Cliffs, N.J.: Prentice-Hall, 1989.
> Contains nearly 200 examples from orchestral literature reduced to four-part score: treble, treble, bass, bass. The last chapter includes full-score movements from symphonies and a Mass.

LANG, C. S. *Score Reading Exercises in Three and Four Parts*, Book I in G and F clefs. London: Novello, 1950. About 80 pages.
> Graded examples of eight to sixteen bars in length, choral style, three and four parts.

————. *Score Reading Exercises in Two, Three, and Four Parts*, Book II in G, F, and C clefs. London: Novello, 1950. 83 pages.
> Carefully graded exercises of twelve to sixteen bars in length. Each includes at least one voice in alto or tenor clef.

MAINOUS, FRANK D. *Melodies to Harmonize With*. Englewood Cliffs, N.J.: Prentice-Hall, 1978. 180 pages.
> Melodies organized by harmony required: I V V7; IV; II; VI; III; modulating to dominant; modulating to relative major/minor; modulating to closely related key; supertonic 7; and so on.

McHose, Allen Irvine, and Ruth Northup Tibbs. *Sight-Singing Manual*. New York: Appleton-Century-Crofts, 1957. 186 pages. Out of print.

> Worthy of searching for because it includes many melodies in C clefs. Excellent for practice of alto and tenor clefs, also for harmonizing melodies in those clefs.

Melcher, Robert O., and Willard F. Warch. *Music for Score-Reading*. Englewood Cliffs, N.J.: Prentice-Hall, 1971. 181 pages.

> Separate chapter of explanation and excerpts for each C clef. Followed by a chapter of excerpts that use that clef for transposition.

Sitt, Hans. *Practical Viola Method*. New York: Carl Fischer, 1924.

> Extended passages for alto clef reading.

Spaeth, Sigmund, and Carl O. Thompson. *55 Art Songs*. Evanston, Ill.: Summy-Birchard, 1943.

> A good collection of accompaniments.

Stanton, Royal. *Steps to Singing for Voice Class*. Belmont, Calif.: Wadsworth, 1983.

> Excellent cross-section of styles and periods for accompaniment practice.